JOYRIDE

JOYRIDE

Tales of First Cars, Classic Cars, and
Dream Cars

THE WRITERS' CACHE

Contents

1. FOREWARD: TO THE OWNER OF THE Z28 CAMARO — 1
Tim Keller

2. SHARK — 5
Nonfiction
Tim Keller

3. BEL AIR SUMMER — 11
Fiction
Jef Huntsman

4. THE YOUTH OF JULY — 26
Poem
Isaac Timm

5. THE 850 CSI — 28
Fiction
Jack Remick

6. EAGLES — 36
Nonfiction
Neil Dabb

7. MECHANIC — 40
Poem
Lynne Burnett

8. TUNES FOR THE ROAD — 42
Nonfiction
Rachel Barham

9. MAKES YOU WONDER — 50
Nonfiction
Marilyn W. Richardson

10. ROAD SHOW — 56
Poem
Jessica de Koninck

11. YOU ALWAYS REMEMBER YOUR FIRST — 58
Nonfiction
J. Anthony Gohier

12. NOT QUITE FLUENT: MY ONGOING EFFORTS
TO MASTER AUTOMOBILE LANGUAGE AND
CULTURE   62
Nonfiction
Felicia Rose

13. I WANT TO ASK YOU   70
Poem
Jessica de Koninck

14. SOAP BOX DERBY   72
Fiction
Stephen Page

15. THE OL' GOAT   76
Nonfiction
Janine Harrison

16. SAUDADE OFF EXIT 32   88
Poem
Kamal E. Kimball

17. THE WHEELS ON THE BUS   90
Nonfiction
Patricia DiMaio

18. ALL THE WAY HOME   97
Nonfiction
Patty Somlo

19. RENTING   107
Poem
Marjorie Maddox

20. WHEELS OF LIFE   109
Nonfiction
Stanley L. Klemetson

21. THE FIRST TIME I SAW HER   113
Nonfiction
S.L. Clarke

22. FULL FENDERED   116
Poem
Michael Langtry

23. CEMENTED   118
Fiction
Keri Montgomery

24. INSECT 131
   Poem
   Fiona Jones

25. ECLIPSE 132
   Fiction
   E.B. Wheeler

26. WILDCAT 149
   Fiction
   Matthew J. Ence

27. ICARUS 1981 159
   Poem
   Isaac Timm

28. HIGH-CENTERED 163
   Nonfiction
   E.B. Wheeler

29. ONE-OH-FIVE 168
   Fiction
   Chadd Van Zanten

ABOUT THE AUTHORS 177

Joyride

Tales of First Cars, Classic Cars, and Dream Cars

Copyright © 2020 The Writers' Cache

Print ISBN: 978-1-7360125-1-2

Front cover image copyright S_Photo via Shutterstock

Back cover image copyright David Phan via Flickr CC BY 2.0

Cover design copyright The Writers' Cache

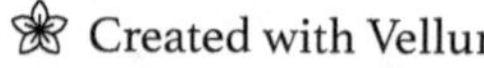 Created with Vellum

FOREWARD: TO THE OWNER OF THE Z28 CAMARO

Tim Keller

IT'S strange how memories and feelings, dormant for years, can be awakened by the least little thing. A long forgotten tune, perhaps, a sight, or even a scent can transport you back.

As I leafed through the Sunday paper over breakfast, I had no idea what lay in store. It was one of those magnificent spring days. It had snowed in the night but the April sun had already melted it away, leaving unseasonable warmth under the brilliant azure sky—and me, luxuriating in the unexpectedly free morning, a snow day for adults.

I normally skip the classifieds but perused them this day in an effort to prolong the mood. In doing so, I noticed an unusually large advertisement, which read, "Wanted, '79 Z28 Camaro."

But not just any Camaro

The author spoke of the '79 Camaro he'd once owned, a car he'd dreamt of and worked toward for years. Finally, in his senior year of high school, his dream came true: a black Z28 with orange racing stripe, straight off the showroom floor, was his. The following year, however, saw hardship in his family and in order to afford to serve a Mormon mission, he was forced to sell his beloved car. But, with every intention of buying it back.

He contacted the buyer when he returned from his mission, only to find the Camaro had been sold, then again, and again. He finally tracked it to a now defunct salvage yard where, miracle of miracles, the owner remembered it had been spared the crusher and sold to "some kid" intent on its restoration.

That was where the trail went cold. Years stretched to decades, until finally, some forty years later, he placed the ad. The serial number of the car was included with a message. He'd pay top dollar, regardless of condition, just to have his car back.

I read and reread the ad. It was a haunting plea. Its brief but powerful appeal, coupled with the almost certain futility of the quest, seized my heart, not with pity or despair, but with wonder and nostalgia. That old angst settled in as the memories swirled. I was thirteen again, riding back from church in my father's Cadillac.

I'd slipped out during services early to admire my cousin Rindy's new car, a gleaming blue Corvette. I'd never seen anything like it. I couldn't look away. This thing didn't have an interior; it had a cockpit, a low slung bucket seat facing a sunken instrument panel with a speedometer that went all the way to 160! I definitely felt the spirit on that day, and it wasn't in the chapel.

Dad interrupted my reverie, hurrying us to the car so as not to be caught behind the line of cars escaping services like second graders at recess. We were free, clear, and doing about 60 down the highway when in the distance, closing from behind like a blue torpedo, appeared Rindy's new Corvette.

In a rare moment of insurrection (Mother did not approve),

Dad, having spied my obvious infatuation, smirked at me through the mirror and pressed the Caddy's accelerator to the floor as Rindy tried to pass. All 501 high-test-gulping cubic inches roared as the Caddy leapt to the occasion until finally, somewhere north of 90, Rindy backed off because of oncoming traffic.

I remember feeling both elated and saddened. Sure the home team had won, and the Caddy was certainly a great car. But Dad took a bit more pleasure in his joke than I thought was sporting.

But then the traffic cleared and again Rindy moved to pass, and again Dad punched it, but to no avail The Stingray might as well have been a fighter jet for all the competition we gave him. I was hooked! So began my unrequited love for muscle cars.

I took to stopping by the dealership every night after my paper route to commune. Until, rather than send me away, they chose to harness my malaise with a weekend detailing job. My favorites were the sports cars. From time to time, they even let me drive—from the lot to the service bay anyway. Alas, my automotive destiny lay elsewhere, and no regrets, but the ache of longing for the road not traveled remains.

Cars were symbols of freedom, power, and status. And they were also in short supply. Most of us had to settle for borrowing our parents' cars, making us betas at best, literally at the mercy of parental whim.

Only slightly better than cars borrowed from parents were the hand-me-downs,

which were almost always old clunkers. Most, parents couldn't afford another car for their teen. Blaine's Impala, for instance, was ancient and slow. To hide the rust, he had repainted the thing baby-blue from a spray can; but hey, at least he had wheels.

But sometimes a kid would get lucky. Many of these so-called family cars were born in the muscle car era. Eric's hand-me-down Chevy station wagon was ugly, but with a Herculean V8 under the hood, it was more than fast enough to compensate for its appearance, and it was big enough for seven or eight of his friends to hang out the many windows, our hair whipping in the wind.

Obviously, the Holy Grail was a car of our own.

Which is where factors like life, means, and needs become ascendant. Where the sometimes painful reality comes crashing in. That not all cars are cool or fast; they're as different as their drivers. For some, cars are symbols of prestige, others, a reflection of personality – there are even those for whom their vehicles are little more than a necessity. A sort of utilitarian symbiosis akin to cowboy and steed.

But from box to dreamboat, clunker to classic, utilitarian to decadent and all points in between, there exists a certain rapport. Cars are more than mere possessions; they are our partners. Is it any wonder we develop attachments to them?

That's what this collection is about. The relationships and experiences related here are as unique as the people who shared them. Perhaps nostalgia will spark a memory or two of your own. A celebration of good times past and those yet to come.

I wonder about the experiences that ad's author and his Z28 must have shared and smile.

Thank you, Sir, for the trip down memory lane. This collection is dedicated to you. I sincerely hope you found your Camaro.

SHARK
NONFICTION
Tim Keller

HEY, remember your first car? I'm not talking about the first one you were allowed to drive. Or the nice one that your sister got to drive. Nor even the one you got stuck with, the one nobody wanted. In my case, that was a rusted-out old Chevy one-ton, heretofore used only for the hauling of hay and live-stock. The embarrassment of being seen in the thing was only slightly eclipsed by the freedom of slipping behind the wheel.

No, I'm talking the first car that was yours, the one you worked and skimped and saved for.

Mine was a brand-new Trans Am.

Or should have been. Four hundred cubic inches of flaming chicken! I was fifteen and had a couple thousand saved up already. Plus, there was another two thousand in the bank, ear-marked for a Mormon mission. I lay awake, all night some-times, scheming to convince the parents to let me spend it. One impossibly elaborate scenario after another kept sleep at bay. When sleep did come, I dreamed of horsepower and the occa-sional rare health condition debilitating enough to keep me out of the mission field yet benign enough to ensure plenty of enjoyment behind the wheel.

That the two bank accounts combined were more than a third of the cost appeared to put the dream within reach. Plus, I had my paper route earnings, which were augmented by summers spent hauling hay (even though I was allergic). And I had my job at the family service station, too, and little by little, the money began to add up.

Then one day in June, the showroom floor of the Palmer Motor Company sported a brand-new Trans Am in Pontiac Cosmos Purple Metallic. I practically flew to the bank, and upon my return, plunked down twenty-five hundred on the spot. Never mind how to pay for the rest.

I won't detail the argument between a boy fighting in earnest for his first love and the soulless orthodoxy of heartless parents who stood in the way. Though I will say I might have had a chance if that idiot salesman hadn't called Mom the moment I walked out the door.

I'll refrain as well, I think, from re-living the humiliation of walking into the dealership to retrieve my twenty-five one hundred dollar bills. I swore I'd never purchase anything from Palmer's. A pact I kept to the day its two locations became an Olive Garden and a vacant lot. Retribution, no doubt karmic in nature, for trifling with the hearts of love-struck boys.

But I digress. This foray into nostalgia is not, after all, about my first mechanical love, but my first car.

Like most soulless minions, Mom and Dad operated under the naive assumption that I'd forget my silly dreams and go back to being a normal kid. Instead, I re-doubled my efforts, taking any odd job I could find. I no longer even deposited my money. Indulging semi-paranoid delusions of parental tyranny, I took to hiding it in clever little places throughout the house. Like the scriptures (no one would ever find it there), under ceiling panels, or couch cushion covers.

I found the last hundred a year or so ago.

And pout? Nothing and no one can brood like a teenager scorned, and even in company so esteemed, I was elite.

"There's no way you could afford the payments," Dad would reason.

"You'd be wrapped around a tree inside a week," Mom would add.

"Or afford the insurance," Dad would say.

"Or the gas," Mom would say.

"We'll help you find another car," Dad promised.

"One you won't wrap around a tree," Mom would add.

But it was no use. What is the power of logic, after all, to the cold and bitter abyss of lost love?

One November Saturday, I was home for lunch when Dad pulled up in an old blue Dodge. He was so proud of himself.

"Now this is how you buy a car," he said. "I serviced this car from the day it rolled off the show room floor. Told the judge every time she came in, if she ever traded up to give me first crack. And now, for five hundred dollars, it's yours."

"I don't want Judge Smith's old car," I snapped.

Dad tossed me the keys.

"Just take her for a spin," he said lazily. "If you still don't want it, I'll keep it for myself."

I'm sure Mom and Dad watched as I huffed outside, but they wisely stayed out of sight. I circled the thing like a prize fighter--this interloper, this consolation prize. I scanned its sleek lines for any imperfection and was all more incensed at finding none.

My fingers traced the freshly waxed surface to the chrome

door handle. The faint scent of lavender wafted over me as I slid behind the wheel.

A grandma car.

"New Yorker" was stenciled on the dash. Twenty-six thousand miles on the odometer. No sign it had ever turned over. I caught a glimpse of curtains moving in the house.

May as well get this over with before they come out, I thought.

I turned the key. The engine fired up at once, smooth and quiet.

"Stupid grandma car," I said, backing out of the drive.

I needed time to think, so I meandered north through town. This was looking more and more unavoidable. Even I couldn't brood forever, and this thing was certainly better than the truck.

Still, a grandma car?

Thoughts of my own grandmother came to mind, and a Sunday dinner less than a year before. The father of one my drivers' ed classmates had donated the use of a Camaro from his dealership for our class. It wasn't a Z28 or anything, just a standard Sport Coupe. Even so, it was a flashy little number that begged to be driven.

Add a talkative and easily distracted teacher, a sunken instrument cluster visible only to the driver and back seat passenger, and a little teamwork on the part of a resourceful group of Stripling Warriors, and a plan which enabled us to more fully appreciate the Camaro was born.

As long as we kept the conversation going, accelerated gradually, and acted all shocked when taking a corner too fast, Mr. Harding didn't suspect a thing. Until we got pulled over, anyway. Man, that cop was pissed! I guess it's not everyday you see a drivers' ed car doing 78 in a 55. Harding was cool about it, by which I mean he didn't flunk us. He did, however, call our parents.

It was all so unfair. I wasn't even driving, and still they went after me. My brother joined in, acting all high and mighty, though he'd certainly done worse and Dad knew it. Even my sister-in-law, no doubt sensing the blood in the water, took her swipes. Mom just kept saying how lucky we were that we hadn't wrapped the car around a tree.

I was just about to launch a suicidal counter attack when Dad interjected with a question.

"Well, Grandma," he drawled. "What do you think about this boy getting a ticket"?

Never mind that no one was ticketed.

The room went silent as all eyes, my own in particular, locked onto our family matriarch. Grandma met my worried glance as she made a show of slipping each finger from her dish-gloves and dropping them gently but decisively onto the table.

"All I can say is, I'm 74 years old. I don't have time to drive the speed limit."

It was true. Grandma, in her 327 Impala, regularly reached 50 mph in the three and a half blocks between her house and ours.

But those 327s are fast. Everyone knows that.

My right foot began to itch with curiosity, and an impression dawned—the idea that New Yorker suffered from a different, though entirely compatible, itch. A single look down the highway showed nothing between Winder and Swan Lake. I smiled.

We surged ahead, New Yorker and I, as the pedal sank to the floor, and in that split second of hesitation as her four massive barrels of carburetor processed an OPEC pleasure-center stimulating blast of high-test, I remember thinking, *This might not be so bad.*

Then the New Yorker gathered her skirts, dropped into passing gear, and launched so hard the cigarette lighter popped from the dash.

Scenery warped into a featureless blur as passing lines solidified. Speedometer numbers I'd previously considered theoretical were eclipsed with astonishing ease until the needle lay bouncing—I shit you not, bouncing—in and out of view at the edge of the speedometer, far beyond the 120 mph hash mark, before finally disappearing under the dash.

Panic set in as every drivers' ed horror film I ever saw flashed before my eyes. But settled almost as fast. Wind roaring? Yes. Tires registering every little pebble? Sure. Even so, we were rock stable. I pulled back on the throttle. Several seconds later, the needle began its descent.

Upon our arrival at home, I lifted the hood and swallowed hard at the words "440 Magnum" and "Police Interceptor" stenciled around the protective drum which circled the air filter.

Gently, even reverently, I closed the hood and circled the car once more. She looked different somehow. Her nose slung slightly lower than the rear. Her low and wide stance gave New Yorker a slightly predatory look. The maw protecting her sunken grill looked so much like a mouth (especially in winter, when icicles hung from the edge) that my younger sister later christened her "The Blue Shark." I couldn't hand Dad his money fast enough.

"Don't tell your mother," he said.

And I don't believe I ever did.

BEL AIR SUMMER
FICTION
Jef Huntsman

EXCITEMENT SURGED through my muscles as we pedaled our bikes six miles from home. Sweat dripped into my fourteen-year-old eyes. I wiped it with my shirttail. New leaves were unfolding on the trees and the city street sweepers hadn't cleaned up winter's grime yet. Wrappers and decayed leaves stuck to the gutters along the lonely road. Soon the gutters ended, gravel and barn grass edged the narrowing asphalt. The two of us braked at a dented, black mailbox that read 2877 Creek Drive in green hand-painted letters.

Lonzo smiled. "Cory, this the place? I don't even see a house let alone a car through these thick trees." I brought Lonzo with me because he's a foot taller, wide as a rhino, has a touch of black stubble on his prominent chin, and was two years older having been held back a couple of grades by his mom. I counted on this age by association. I needed all the help I could get to look old enough to buy a car.

I nodded and straightened my spine, hoping my 4' 11" gangly frame would make me older. My blonde stringy hair covered my ears and duck-tailed down over my blue T-shirt. I thought about lighting up a Winston, but then if he's Mormon, like most people here, it might give him reason not to sell. Didn't need that. Lonzo and I had left our Stingray bikes in the high spring weeds by the mailbox where a pounded gravel path made way for the new weeds which lined the sides and middle. I choked from anticipation and fear as we rounded a corner and spotted the car.

It was the spring of 1966; this wasn't the first car I'd bought but it was the first one I was hoping to buy alone. There were twelve of us that had gone in on two other cars. None of us were old enough for a driver's license. Back then, for cash, most of us saved lunch money. Two guys had paper routes and Harrison sold bags of Spudnuts, a popular donut mix of potatoes, sugar, and flour, door to door. Today, my pocket bulged from a wad of cash I'd earned on Saturdays at my dad's auto repair shop.

My eyes widened. A 1953 Bel Air waited for us only twenty feet away. All curved lines and heavy metal in a light blue with a bumper that could stop a rhino. We started up the path, I glanced over and smiled at Lonzo.

"You the boys?" came a raspy voice behind the car.

I startled. "What?"

"You the boys that called about the Chevy?"

A tall, thin man with sun-wrinkled walnut skin stood by the car leaning on a cottonwood tree with a beer can in his hand. He spit to the side as if irritated at the sight of me.

My tongue stuck to the top of my mouth. I nodded and headed toward the car. Lonzo followed.

The Chevy had wide whitewall tires and chrome that reflected the morning sun. The hood ornament had been stolen, the antenna was snapped off, and the driver's side vent mirror had a spider crack. None of that was a deterrent. I stuck my head in the open window. Black tuck and roll seats, radio with one knob missing, and a clock that had the right time. I had to have this!

I backed my neck out the window and turned. The tall, thin man tossed me a set of keys.

"Start her up." His eyes had changed. Friendly, but now with a hint of sadness.

The motor roared to life. I beamed and held on to that giant round steering wheel. I leaned to my right and checked all the dials as if I knew what they did, opened the glove box, stared at an owner's manual, a few bottle caps, and glanced at some folded papers laying inside, then slid the ashtray in and out as if checking something as important as the oil.

"The hood latch is down there." The thin, tall man pointed through the window.

I nodded.

After a thick moment, the thin, tall man raised his voice a touch, "Ya want to look under the hood?"

"Uh, yeah." I hurriedly popped the latch, opened the door, and slid out. Lonzo followed me to the front.

We stared at the motor and nodded. I knew three things about cars: they needed gas and oil, they were a hoot to drive, and if something didn't work you took it to a mechanic or in my case on the previous community car, left it on the side of the road and walked home. But the engine ran and there didn't seem to be any black liquids spurting out anywhere. I wanted it.

I closed the hood and turned to the man. "I know in the paper you were asking for $300, but I only got $253.28." I bit my bottom lip. "Any way you could take that?"

The man's chin began to quiver, and his once stern eyes watered up. He bowed his head and turned away. He began sobbing.

Panic started at the top of my head and flowed downward. My left foot tapped on the gravel. "I could, uh, work off the rest." My voice raised an octave, and I glanced around the property. "Maybe do something around here or work at my dad's shop and pay you weekly?"

Lonzo reached through the window and turned the Chevy off. The only sounds were the man's low blubbering and two birds singing from the willow tree.

I stood still not knowing what to do or say. Had I offended him? I thought about running back to our bikes and peddling away as fast as we could. I glanced at Lonzo. He shrugged then focused on the ground.

The man finally took in a deep breath, wiped his cheeks on his sleeve, and turned back to us. His eyes were red and hollow. He pulled at the skin on his Adam's apple and rubbed the front of his teeth with his tongue. In a soft voice he said, "Sorry boys." He paused for some time. "This was my son's car. His body just returned from Vietnam ten days ago." He took long draw of air in and let it out slowly. "Whatever you got. I just want the damn thing out of here."

My feet shuffled. This was awkward. I reached in my pocket and pulled out the roll of cash with a rubber band around it and handed it to him. I reached back in for the change, he shook his head.

"The title's in the glove box already signed. Now git." The thin, tall man walked away with shoulders drooped.

My throat tightened for a few seconds. I watched the shaken man hobble up his porch stairs. The thrill of owning a Chevy Bel Air took over. With a grin, I hopped in and admired the console. One hand grasp the steering wheel while the other slipped in the key and turned. My chest puffed up like those birds trying to attract a mate.

I stopped at the entrance of his property, and Lonzo tossed the bikes in the trunk. We were off, windows down, hair blowing in the wind, and my eyes focusing on the road between the top of the steering wheel and the dash.

Within an hour, we had packed in six other friends and headed for the canyon. Windows down with elbows out, spring air drifting across long locks, and the flash of the sun through the trees. We were at the top of our game. The Bel Air glided around every corner. We drove up and down the canyon twice hooting at picnickers on the side of the road.

As an edge of darkness hit, I felt that kick to my brain warning: *Mom's watching the clock with dinner ready, plates laid out, and her number two son's not home. I may buy a car without her ever knowing but being late for dinner was the eighth deadly sin.* I hurried home.

Parking in front of a vacant lot, we jumped out and headed home. The keys felt good in my pocket. I rode my bike over to the top of the next street, parked on my lawn, and burst through the screen door to find everyone sitting at the table waiting. Mom sucked in her lips and did that crinkle thing with her forehead. I bowed my head and marched straight for my place at the table. Mom nodded, and we all began eating. Not a word was said, but I hurt as if she'd given me lashes with a willow branch—which never happened—though the threat was always there. My sister and brother smiled. I gave back a gruff look. Silverware clattered on plates until all plates were empty. I knew what was coming.

"Cory, you're on dishes tonight. After that, check with Dad on where the house needs scrapping before we paint."

Oh well, I had a new car. I kept feeling the key in my pocket. Man, I wanted to go drive it all night.

"What's with the grin?" Mom glanced at Dad. "He's done something."

"Why were you late, son?"

Lying never worked with them. I've got to remember not to touch my face. That's a giveaway and damn, quit biting your lip. "Just out riding bikes with Lonzo."

Dad's eyes narrowed. He waited.

I was sure he could hear my heart crashing against my ribs like cymbals.

His face softened. "Okay. The scrappers in the garage. Use the three-inch one, not the putty knife."

"Am I getting paid for this?"

Mom's neck jutted toward me. Her eyes bore through a spot on my forehead.

I held up my palms. "I'm happy to do it for the family." I jammed the last glob of meatloaf in my mouth and stood. "I'll go find the scrapper."

Mom smiled using the one that came and went so fast you'd think she worked the counter at the Dairy Queen.

The next day I was on the family project of painting the house and all I could think about was wrapping my hands around the steering wheel of my new Bel Air. But first, I had to make it legal and not get pulled over by an overzealous cop. I needed license plates, and I knew just the place to get them.

Late that night, I snuck out through my bedroom window and met Lonzo. We headed out to borrow the plates off Mrs. Anderton's 1960 Desoto that sat in her garage collecting dust. She was on a Church mission to Peru or Pakistan, one of the "P" countries, helping poor people brush their teeth or something. By the time she got back the plate would be expired anyway, and it would be returned.

The garage wasn't locked as I assumed. With a slow push,

the lift-up door squealed like dusty brakes. Lonzo stuck a board under the edge after I lifted the door about a foot up. Broken cobwebs draped from the rubber seal down to earthen floor like black doilies. I laid on my side and shined the flashlight. A white beam reflected off the chrome front. Waving the light, I spotted our goal–– a Utah AY1733 with an expiration in October. I did the math in my head. Plates good for another seven months. With a smirk, I slid under the door. Lonzo followed with plyers and a screwdriver. I dusted the webs from my face and arms in a spastic shiver, then went to work unscrewing the license plates.

I heard Lonzo as he opened the door to the Desoto and scooted behind the wheel. Soon, he was fiddling with every knob and button on the dash. I undid the rear plate and moved to the front.

"Keys are in the ashtray," bellowed Lonzo.

"Great, leave them and don't touch anything." I twisted the second screw.

The starter motor whined as 295 HP came to life pumping eight cylinders up and down. The front end lifted as Lonzo stepped on the gas. I dropped the screwdriver, fell backwards, spun around, and ran towards the driver's door, ripped the door open with one hand, reached around the steering wheel, and spun the keys. The motor gurgled, then quieted.

"Are you nuts. It's one in the morning." I grabbed Lonzo, who was at least thirty pounds heavier than me and yanked him out of the seat, banging his head on the door. He fell to the ground.

His eyes narrowed. His bulky arm muscles tightened. A rage dropped over his face.

"Lonzo, Lonzo, calm." I stood, raised my hands––palms out. "Just calm, okay?" I had seen this face before. He once picked up a kid older and bigger than him, above his head, and tossed him like an empty pop can into thorny pyracantha bushes because the boy called him stupid. I spoke in soft tones while backing up slightly. He rose to his knees. I sucked in air through my teeth ready to sprint away.

"I'm sorry, but what if the neighbors heard that?" I carefully grabbed his tense bicep. "We've got to get out of here." His muscles slowly relaxed. Relief washed over me. It was good I was his best friend.

I found my tools on the ground, spun off the last screw, and grabbed the plates. We rolled under the door and listened for signs of anyone coming. The silence was settling. I yanked the board and the door dropped into place. We ran to where I'd left the car that day and I tightened on the plates. We were legal—at least in my mind.

———

The next morning, I bounced out of bed with purpose, slipped on Levi shorts, the ones with an iron-on patch on the butt and an inch of dangling threads over my thighs, a T, and black Keds sneakers. I reached in the closet and shook my Sunday shoes until the car keys fell into my open hand. They went into my pocket. A drive to the lake was on my agenda. I floated on air down to the kitchen. The sounds of family chatter and the smell of bacon and maple syrup hit me. I thought I'd gotten up early, but these people rise with the sun in the summer. What's up with that? After filling up on eggs and hotcakes, I was lucky. Mom only needed me to take out the trash.

I called Lonzo and then Gayla on the party line. Knowing any of four houses, or worse my sister who couldn't keep a secret even if she didn't know it, could listen in on my conversation. I kept both calls short.

"Be at the corner in ten minutes. The great and powerful Mr. Bel Air will be waiting." I felt like 007.

I pulled up to where Lonzo and Tick were standing. The street was empty. Hoses with sprinklers waved back and forth, dotting the neighborhood lawns, and dogs broke the silence in barked calls from front porches and behind chain-link fences. Gayla and her friend Mary Lynn came around the corner off Harrison Street. Gayla wore a floral pantsuit and Mary Lynn had on a white peasant blouse and a black and white striped pencil skirt.

I motioned Lonzo and Tick into the back seat with my thumb. Lonzo pushed a tuft of black hair from his eyes and squinted hard with displeasure, then glanced at the girls and nodded. We waited while the girls took their time walking down the sidewalk, leaning in to say something to each other then giggling with a skip.

I roared the engine to get them to hurry. That got the dogs barking like crazy—the girls never varied their pace.

"What's this got in it?" asked Tick. Aurelius Tickerman was a husky, round-headed kid with a face that was more nose than anything else, and glasses powerful enough to burn ants. *What sort of parents name their kid Aurelius?*

My chest puffed. "215 cubic inch with six cylinders of pure power."

"How fast will she fly?" Tick asked.

"It moves. I'm sure she'll do a hundred."

"I dig it!"

Gayla opened the door and slid in next to me. Mary Lynn took shotgun.

Gayla was my girlfriend. Well, there was never anything

said. It was just known between the two of us. We'd been best friends since we were five. A few years back, we changed from playing street games to sneaking into her basement and kissing until our lips were raw. I liked the latter.

I punched the gas. Gravel spit from the wheels and the rear end fishtailed into the road. I'd pulled that off as if running Daytona.

"Far out car." Gayla gave me a look and that sweet smile.

I gave it a touch more gas and glanced at what the girls were wearing. "You know we're going to the lake?"

"Swimsuit's underneath. You thought I could leave my house in a two piece? My mom would freak."

I nodded approval.

After a quick stop at 7-11 for necessities, drinks, pringles, licorice ropes and Ding Dongs, we shot up I-80 to the lake. The Bel Air glided up Parleys Canyon shifting to the right on bouncy shocks and a broken rear spring. Our laugher echoed through the car.

The exit came up fast, the car swerved to the right then fishtailed down the ramp, and I quickly found out how well the brakes worked. Everyone in the front slid forward, hands shot out to cushion our momentum––Lonzo and Tuck nose-dived into the back of the front seat. Tuck got a bloody nose that we used a ratty old shop rag to stop. The rest of us were fine.

The lake was filled with snow melt and cold enough to keep popsicles. Gayla and I made-out while the other three dangled their feet in the water and talked of important nonsense.

Hours later, the sun and fired up emotions sweated Gayla and me out of the car. I slipped off my shoes, ran past my friends and jumped into the icy lake. Gasping for breath as my skin turned blue, I swam to shore, raced to the Bel Air, and laid chest down on the hood for heat as if trying to make love to a hunk of metal. No one else followed my lead.

Mary Lynn held out her watch to me as I lay on the hood. "I've got dance in an hour."

"We better go," stated Gayla.

The Bel Air roared to life and we were off. The road was narrow and curved. It circled the lake on a raised strip of pecan-colored dirt with thick quakies on the right and water on the left. That big steering wheel made the driving easy. The car cornered the dirt road as if floating on wings. On the third turn, with dust billowing from the tires, the rear door flung open and Lonzo rolled out like a bundled possum. A ball of blue shirt and crunched legs bounced across the ground coming to rest against a white tree trunk with a thud.

My foot stomped on the brake and we swerved to a stop. A fog of dust lifted.

Lonzo's hair and shoulders were splayed on the ground facing us covered in dust and dry leaves. His feet wrapped to one side of the trunk at a sick angle. Our treat bag had been flung and scattered Pringles like confetti across the bank to his left.

Mouths hung open. *Alive?* was the question no one dared ask. We waited. Gayla finally broke the silence and called through the open window, "Lonzo . . . Lonzo?"

I came out of my shock, ripped open the door, and ran over to where he lay. The others followed.

His eyes, wide open, looked dazed. Three crimson cuts paralleled down his right cheek as if pointing to the oval scrap of skin on his chin. He breathed in a sharp gasp. "What the hell?"

"You okay?" I asked.

His arms lifted. "Help me up."

Tick unwound Lonzo's legs from the tree trunk, and I eased him to his feet. He padded dust from his shirt and shorts. He was careful around the scraped knees.

Holding him by his armpits, I asked, "Can you stand?"

His body jerked out of my grip. "I'm fine." He laughed as he bent down and retrieved a dusty Pringle. "I'm not sitting by that door." He popped the Pringle in his mouth.

"Gross." Mary Lynn crinkled her nose.

"It must have not been shut all the way," I said.

"Bullshit, you lean against it. I'll drive." He began hobbling over to the driver's side.

"Nobody but me drives. Besides, you can barely walk." I opened the rear door, got in, and slammed it shut. With my back against the seat, my feet on the door panel, knees bent, I pushed on the door. "See, nothing happens."

"Let me drive?" he whined.

I gave one good kick to the inside of the door. The hinge clicked and the door swung open. Birds squawked in the tree above us. I rolled up and slid through the door. "Just don't lean on it."

Gayla, Mary Lynn and Tick laughed. Lonzo crossed his arms in defiance.

"Let me help." Mary Lynn took him by the hand over to the lake's grassy shore and patted his cuts and scrapes with the cool water, washing tiny streams of blood away. Lonzo beamed from the attention.

With Lonzo settled, we headed down the mountain to the city. He sat in the middle as if someone were to the right of him. His hands clutched the seat.

I parked the Bel Air in the church parking lot. It was the safest place to park an illegally- bought car, though I knew I would have to move it around to different parking spaces every night so no one would call it in as an abandoned car. I was positive an impound lot wouldn't release my Bel Air to a kid whose only form of ID was a student card from Wasatch Junior High. On the walk home, I mentioned I needed a driver's license.

I'll grab my brother's from his wallet. He loses it all the time," said Mary Lynn as if stealing was no different than passing the potatoes at dinner.

Problem solved.

As we followed the sidewalk home past freshly-mowed lawns and sweet smells of meals being prepared, Lonzo tapped me from behind on the shoulder. I turned.

"You need to have the car painted," Lonzo said excitedly. "That sky blue is a bummer. The Bel Air deserves something bad––something far out."

I never thought of that. I nodded in agreement. "That'd be cool." By the time I got home, I knew what was going to happen. I phoned a bunch of friends to help me the following Monday.

At noon on Monday, eight friends showed up, including Tick and Lonzo, to the far corner of the Grand Central store parking lot. I had a week's worth of newspapers, masking tape from our garage, and two grocery sacks filled with gold aerosol spray paint. With newsprint taped over the windows, wheels, and chrome, we began shaking and spraying the Bel Air until it gleamed like a metallic golden goddess. After sitting an hour catching some rays, we took off the masking. A few runs and a couple of ripples faded into the new look. The nine of us stood back and admired the gold beast. Incredible. We especially loved the orange-peel look we'd somehow accomplished without even knowing how to do it.

Like gladiators after a battle, we drove up and down State

Street showing off the new look. People stared; some pointed. Envy was easy to read.

That summer the golden Bel Air took Lonzo, Gayla, Mary Lynn, and Tick to the drive-in to watch Fantastic Voyage, Our Man Flint, and Fahrenheit 451. It curved up the canyon for hot-dog picnics and evening parking dates. The four of us plus two other friends rode in the Bel Air downtown to march in two equal-rights protests and to the Terrace ballroom to see the Lovin' Spoonful, The Troggs, and The Who in concert. We drank beer and smoked weed. I drove everyone around way before taking any drivers ed. I'm not sure if we were rebels or just kids having a blast.

One night when we were driving home, flashing lights came on behind us. Muscles tensed. I ignored the blue and red flash in my rearview mirror.

"Oh my God. Oh my God," Gayla squealed.

That didn't help. I gave it a touch more gas. A short burst of siren penetrated my ears. My arms were shaking. My throat tightened to where I wasn't sure if I could breathe. In panic, I floored the gas. The Bel Air roared and tires squealed as we raced down the street. I watched the police car get further and further away. My teeth clamped on my lower lip. Gayla was screaming. I skidded around a corner, glanced in the rearview mirror, and saw blackness. Then the full siren came on.

I spotted a vacant lot to my left. In fear, I cranked the wheel. The car fishtailed, then straightened and bounced over the curb, through shoulder-high weeds. Clicking the lights off, I grasped the steering wheel with all my might and pointed the front end between two trees about thirty feet apart. The siren roared on the street behind us.

Just as I let off the gas to hide in the tall brush, we sailed in weightless abandon. The steering went slack. The front end dipped and dropped into black oblivion. The engine roared. Then we hit ground, bounced like riding a bull, and slammed into something solid. I had braced on the steering wheel. Gayla's arms were outstretched to the dash. The force folded our arms. Our bodies hurled forward and crashed into the dash and then flung us back against the tuck and roll seats. My knee bumped the lights on. The motor stalled. Headlights beamed through a cloud of dust.

I glanced at Gayla. Her mouth hung open. I tried to turn around to see how Tick and Lonzo were doing. Intense pain stopped me. I laid my head back on the seat.

I moved my arms and legs to make sure everything worked. "Everyone okay?" I whispered.

Gayla sat up and smacked me. I dabbed the blood from her lip with my shirttail. She glared.

"That was a bummer," said Lonzo. "I'm fairly sure we're okay. Bruised tomorrow though."

"I think you lost the cop," said Tick.

I opened my door and helped Gayla slide over and out my side. She was mad but not mad enough to stay in the car. Tick slid out his side. Lonzo rammed his door.

"Now the door stays shut." Lonzo laughed.

The four of us climbed out and gazed around. It appeared to be a dug-out hole for a basement. We helped each other climb out then hobbled the six blocks home.

That warm night I left my golden Bel Air in that hole and never went back, but it always gave me a grin to think about my first real car and the summer it gave me.

4

THE YOUTH OF JULY
POEM

Isaac Timm

GIRL of fifteen hangs out the window,
    slender arm waving like a moth
    at a friend passing or past,
    her escort a phantom young
    man from the nose down, eyes
    lost to the glare.

The street flows with the youth of July,
    some to eddy into parking lots, pieces
    of green yard, spread on blankets,
    piled on tailgates. Laughter, like bells
    over bass, caught in small moments between
    the passing of cars, a cavalcade of tanned elbows
    and flashing faces under a halo of bangs.
    Pretty smiling girls to be lost then discovered,
    passing and turning, crossing in and out of lanes.

· · ·

Sex rumbles in the heart like an engine,
    a slow present backbeat happening below sheltering
    cottonwoods, under lap throws, flush young faces,
    fumbling hands groping as if ecstasy can be lost,
    to flow endlessly to the east out of town, with
    honking traffic and now headlights.

Evening casts its self out. Beer cans come out of hiding,
    from under daddy's gun rack, from behind mama's quilt,
    down on the floor-board. And they drink until midnight,
    until dispersed by unseen hands. Replaced by empty street,
    a single slow squad car, neon that winks "closed."
    But somewhere is a rumble under the street lamps,
    the promise of another Friday night.

5

THE 850 CSi
FICTION

Jack Remick

I SAT IN THE PICKUP. Mel had the wheel. At two-thirty the house lights had been off for half an hour and Dr. Johnson's BMW 760Li lay in a shaft of light—yellow and blue and silver and glass. Dr. Cynthia Johnson was a long-legged, blonde-headed, silicon-queen surgeon who chopped the fat out of LA beauties and rebuilt them into sleek, smooth, big-boobed beach honeys.

Acid was chewing a hole in my gut so I shuffled through the glove box hunting for the Tums.

"Relax, Jonny," Mel said. "It's just a car."

"You do it then," I said.

I shook out three Tums and chewed them and waited until the burning cooled and then I stepped out of the pickup, strapped on the webbed tool belt with the electric screwdrivers and the socket set and the wire cutters.

Crossing under the light, my footsteps crunched on the sandy concrete. I expected alarms to go off and lights to come on, but when I stopped there was just the thrum of swimming pool pumps and the faint buzz of the night. I slid under the 760, reached up into the fender panel and with the cutters, cut the by-pass I had patched in while the car was in the shop. The 760's alarm was now dead. After that, you could do anything to her you wanted. I keyed the car, opened the door and got behind the wheel.

Across the street, Mel started the pickup and drove away.

At the shop on Pacific Coast Highway, I ran the 760 into Bay 1 and shut her down.

———

I hated Mel right then. I hated the business Mel was in. I hated myself for letting Mel suck me into his penny-ante pissant crime scheme. In Bay 1 I would gut the 760. I would take her apart piece by piece down to the instrument panel until she lay spread out, butchered, her near-new parts gleaming raw bones in the neon overheads. At first it was easy, even a little bit of a thrill, but now, every time I cut into a car I got sick to my stomach.

While I slaughtered and boned the 760, while I waited for Mel to show up, I remembered the day he had called me into his office. I was in the shop finishing up a rush chip job on an Audi TT. It was around quitting time. Maybe 6:30. Mel was sitting at the metal desk, head down, like a man praying, but even then I knew Mel prayed to just three gods—Money, Women, and Doobie.

He reared back, braced his smooth black clean-shaven head between his thick hands and said,"Jonny, I'm gonna let you go."

"What? I'm not getting the work done?"

"You're getting the work done fine."

He got out of his chair, went to the shop window. Standing there, he looked like he could tear the lug nuts off a BMW with his bare teeth. Mel's a big guy and if you look at just his size you'd cross the street before you'd brush up close to him. Out in the shop, the Audi TT was up on the rack, its electrics spread out like the guts of metal animal just butchered.

"What's going on then, dude?"

"Dude," he said, "no one's called me dude in a while."

"You're letting me go because I call you dude?"

"I'm going broke, Jonny."

"Broke?"

"Yeah. Broke. I'll close the shop if things don't shape up."

"You want me to work for free."

He laughed. He sat down in his chair, elbows on the desk, and he snapped open an Altoids mint box and fingered a rolled joint that he lit and took a hit on and he held the smoke in then let it out in short jerks.

"I need some help and it doesn't look like you're the man."

"What's eating you?"

He bogarted the joint, leaned back in his chair.

"I owe some people some money that I don't have and I can't get."

"I've got a few bucks," I said. "What do you need?"

"Eighty."

"Eighty. I can swing that."

"Eighty grand," he said.

I looked out the door of the shop to where the Audi TT sat in its Toledo blue crystal paint, smooth and sloped so you could almost see the wind splitting over the shell and I remembered once out on the Santa Monica freeway watching an 850 CSi chase a Ferrari like a wolf after a calf, lights flashing, horn blaring and the BMW blew past. I was sitting on 120 but he made me look like I'd blown a piston and froze up the engine. There in the shop the TT looked like a blue arrow. I didn't know it was aimed at my heart. I looked at Mel. Then at the car.

"These sons of bitches want meat, Jonny. If they don't get their money they cut my nuts off and stuff 'em in my mouth."

Mel had sweat on his face. I smelled the cannabis on him.

I owed Mel. I'd owed him for a long time. He held out a hand to me when I didn't know a torque converter from a jackrabbit and he'd let me work overtime and gave me clients who wanted me to chip their engines to tweak another fifty horsepower out of their stock mills. And then Mel glared at me.

"What?"

"I need a man who can use his tools in the right place at the right time and keep his mouth shut after he does it. Jonny, you know every secret code on these things."

You know how it is when you're in the dark and you feel something crawl up your back? That's the way it was when Mel looked at me then. I felt creepy. Crawly. Dirty.

I knew what he wanted all right, and it felt sacrilegious.

"What are you asking me, Mel?"

"I got a guy in TJ. He wants that TT. Wednesday morning."

"You want me to run that TT to Mexico?"

"He pays cash."

"You know what'll happen to it in TJ," I said. "They'll gut it and skin it and chop it for parts."

"Not this guy. He wants the car. Whole. Look, Jonny. You don't care. Mr Franz don't care, I don't give a shit. Insurance covers it all anyway."

———

I came back from TiJuana on a bus. I hadn't been on a bus in a long time. Taxied from the Greyhound to PCH. The taste of the

Greyhound stayed in my mouth until I got a lungful of ocean breeze.

———

Dr Johnson's 760 looked like Edward Scissorhands had chewed on it by the time Mel showed up. Grinning. Half-whacked. A joint glued to his lips. He walked around the 760 the way Patton did in that movie where he surveys the bodies in the desert after a tank battle.

"You're good, Jonny," he said. "Damn, you are good."

"This is the last one, Mel. I finish this one, I quit."

"It's not that easy, J Boy," he said.

Everything went to hell when he told me we were going to chop Ms Redman's 850 CSi.

———

I'm barely two months on Mel's payroll the first time I meet Beatrice Redman. I'm young and stupid so I don't know I'm on a cold slide to murder. You can't tell by looking. She drives her BMW 850 CSi into Mel's Shop on PCH. She's tall and thin. Black pants, black top, a white wrap you can almost see through. And you notice that she looks hungry. No big deal. A lot of women in LA look hungry.

BMW. Black. The back end has a ding the size of a football crushing in the BMW logo. I feel like someone's crushed me. Yanked my heart out. An 850 CSi is as close to perfection as anything humans can ever make. I look at her. She smiles at me. A killer smile. She's hell on wheels. You get a woman's number just like that. You smell the hell-fire, see the ashes in the eyes, but you can't look away. You like fire. You want her to jam a smoldering cigarette to your nipple. Anything. It's going to hurt. So what? Simple.

"Who did this?"

"When can you have it fixed?"

"A couple of days," I say.

"You're new here, aren't you?"

"I'm new."

"What's your name?"

"Jonny Wattron. No H."

"Jonny. No H." She says it like it's a mouthful of cotton candy.

I check over the BMW. Run her through the computer.

58 Via Campesina, Palos Verdes Estates. 1996. 850 CSi. Only 38,000 miles. Not even a scuff on the accelerator and brake pedals. Leather smells almost new. As I do the paperwork, I watch her. I try not to notice the quiver in the lips. The skin is tanned, but her face isn't lined. She's maybe 40, but like her car, she's in good shape. The sun makes her glisten. The mileage makes her a mystery.

"Well, I think it's gonna run you close to two grand."

"What?" she says.

"About two grand. To fix this up. The insurance."

"I am my own insurance," she says. "Should I just throw it away and buy a new one?" That smile again. Red mouth. White teeth. Very white teeth.

That was a Monday morning. Monday afternoon. I strip and patch the ding. The dent eats three layers of fiberglass before it smooths out. Tuesday morning I sand and prime. Tuesday afternoon I match the midnight black from BMW. And paint it. Laying on the paint, watching it curve to the panel. A second coat of black and three coats of lacquer and you can't tell she ever backed into whatever it was she backed into.

Wednesday afternoon I call her.

She answers. Asks if I can bring it out.

Mel says Ms Redman is good for it. He gives me taxi fare. We tack it on the bill.

We close Wednesday evening at 7:00. By 7:10 I'm driving PCH to Palos Verdes Estates. It's a cool night. Sunset already dying. You see the lights along PCH like sparklers and the rusty layer of sky on the horizon, LA red—a burnt orange hovering over the black line of the Pacific Ocean. The air is still. It's paradise in the BMW. The CSi talks to me. All the way. I love cars that talk. Big. Fast. Powerful. Comfortable. Rich. Leather. The she-smell of perfume and money and the dull odor of cigarettes.

For a couple of beats I'm at a stoplight and I look at the car next to me and Miss Southern California smiles and I smile back and I know she doesn't blink if I'm in a Chevy or a Ford, even my chopped Ford. But an 850. Well.

I want it.

Palos Verdes Estates is everything LA should be—winding hill-side streets lined with eucalyptus trees and jacaranda and on the slopes, neo-Spanish castles built of white brick and red tile roofs that glisten in the sunset melting down over the Pacific Ocean.

When you turn a close curve, peacocks with their rainbow fans screech at you like they own the place.

Later she tells me about the peacocks—how someone let them loose and how they took over and now perch on rooftops and how they breed and how much she loves them and how if anyone killed one of them, she'd have him skinned alive. I pull into the drive at 58 Via Campesina, a curved drive big enough to hold a herd of German cars and I shut down the mill of the 850 CSi and I hear the birds chittering and the peacocks call and I hear the long slow whine of swimming pool pumps and some-where, in another universe, a crow caws. And for a second I forget who I am and where I am and what I am doing because for just that second I have a feeling for what it would be like to come to a place like that every day with its peacocks on the roof and a swimming pool that hums and inside a woman who wears black and white and drives a big fast powerful rich German machine. I think about home, the futon I sleep on, the breakfast of raisin bran and cold coffee. I get out of the car.

The garage door rolls up, a slow, mechanical chugging, and there, in front of a shiny black Jaguar stands Bea Redman in black pants and white blouse with a pearl choker. Her hair looks like the wings of a big bird.

She rubs her hand over the trunk lid. You see her skin mirrored in the lacquer. The woman and the car—sleek, smooth, dangerous. She looks at me. "It looks like new," She says.

After she inspects the BMW, she stands back like an arts patron measuring the value of black and white in an expensive wall piece. She smells good. Fresh like a rose in high bloom wanting to be plucked.

6

EAGLES
NONFICTION
Neil Dabb

IN THE 80'S TV series *Airwolf,* a beautiful test pilot named Roan tells the protagonist, Stringfellow Hawke, that when she was young, she dreamed of flying with a pair of eagles who nested near her house. With her P-51 Mustang fighter-plane, she finally felt she could join them. When her plane is destroyed, Hawke tells her there will be other eagles. She says, "No. We only get one. After that they are only airplanes."

I believe the same could be said of cars.

I grew up with Saturday morning cartoons and watched the series "Hot Wheels." I have vivid memories of setting up the Hot Wheels tracks I'd get for Christmas and running the tiny racecars around the track. With the self-powered *Sizzler* cars I could set up a track that was almost as long as the house in the backyard and watch that little car do laps. I imagined that I was driving to high-speed adventure.

Long before turning sixteen, I was driving pickup trucks around the hay fields and later cars on the back-roads near my home. When I finally turned sixteen I had nearly free reign of an old white Plymouth Fury III four-door sedan. Though I didn't recognize it at the time, I had found my Eagle. With that car I could squeal the tires for half a block and keep accelerating until I ran out of road. A buddy of mine had a Dodge with the same engine, a 383 V8, and after school we would chase each other around the roads near our high school under the guise of going home.

It was only after my parents sold the car because the transmission was failing that I realized what I'd had. I've compared every car I've ever owned or driven to that old Plymouth Fury III: *My Eagle.* My time working at the local service station after my parents sold the Plymouth taught me just enough to bluff my way through any discussion my friends and I might have about cars. It also taught me what I lost when my parents chose to sell my Eagle. Among other things, I learned that the Chrysler 383 engine was popular among racers, and particularly those with the four-barrel carburetor like my Plymouth Fury III had. I also learned that the four-barrel carburetor got better gas mileage than the less powerful, two-barrel versions (assuming you kept your foot out of the gas).

After serving a mission for the Church of Jesus Christ of Latter Day Saints, I married. My father-in-law owned a Ford Mustang. Once when I was driving him home in his car after dropping his other car at the mechanic, we pulled up to a stop sign and the smart-alec next to us revved his engine. The Mustang left him in the dust, and when I looked at my father-in-law he had a Cheshire cat grin on his face. Later after he had bought a newer Mustang, I borrowed it for a week or so while our car was in the shop. One night that week I drove the car to the rocket factory where I worked. That night I followed a friend, a part-time cop who drove the same model of Mustang as that of my father-in-law, home. The difference between the

Mustangs was that my friend's had a 5.0 V8, while my father-in-law's Mustang had the standard engine. I pulled up beside my friend at a deserted stop sign and revved the engine. I matched him gear for gear till we hit 55 MPH. Then he left me in the dust. My Plymouth Fury III could've matched him till we ran out of road.

My children have made a habit of naming the cars we drive. Typically, they pick names that match the attitude of the car (or that give the car attitude). The red Chevy Astro van I bought to take to work was named Max. Max had a lot of power off the line, which we appreciated when my wife and I spent a week or two every summer attending conferences around the country. In Chicago, for example, driving is like a constant drag race. I would drive my wife to the conference so that between sessions we could see the sights. The Fury would've done great there, especially with a load of amplifiers and guitars in the trunk; a fact I learned during the short time I played bass guitar in my dad's western band. That extra weight was just enough to keep from melting the tires for half a block. Max, like the Fury, was eventually retired after my children began driving it to school.

Beast was a work vehicle that had power off the line reminiscent of my Plymouth Fury III. During my time working at the service station I learned that many of the four-wheel drive vehicles my friends drove could beat the racers off the line because of the low-end torque. Even when dragging a thirty-foot trailer full of equipment, Beast could still pass the big trucks that were running empty. Like Beast, my Plymouth Fury III had power to spare.

In my youth, I found joy in driving cars in the winter, particularly in empty slick parking lots. For the first few winters that I could drive legally, I would find an empty, usually un-plowed, parking lot and cut donuts or spin out whatever vehicle I could.

The first car I did this in was my Plymouth Fury III, my Eagle. These skills became so second nature that I would sometimes forget that I was compensating while driving down the roads, until I tried to stop.

Four-wheel drive vehicles are supposedly the ultimate for handling snow, but I have since learned that this is not always the case. It was in Beast that I learned that four-wheel drive vehicles are not invincible. I was on my way to Salt Lake on an early snowy morning, and I had put Beast in four-wheel drive. This worked well on the uphill side of Sardine canyon, but shortly after topping the summit I tried to slow down and spun out. Once I got Beast back under control, I took it out of four-wheel drive and had no problems the rest of the trip. My Eagle, my Plymouth Fury III, never spun out on me (unless, of course, I wanted her to).

Today there are cars with computers that have more power than the computers used to send man to the moon. There are cars that can go faster than the old-time racers with much smaller engines. But in the end they are only cars. We only get one Eagle, and mine was an old Plymouth Fury III with a 383 V8 engine.

7

MECHANIC
POEM

Lynne Burnett

NOT YOUR STANDARD GUY—PUT a shift kit
in the automatic transmission of his
Boyd Red 1990 Ford Mustang LX 5.0
coupe, changed the seats from black
vinyl to cloth: *made it turn-on-a-dime
crazy 'round a corner, full-out perfect
snort of heaven off a light and down
highway 99. No one could catch me,*
he grins, *unless I wanted them to.*

Nothing mechanical in the way he bends
over the lifted hood of my car or lays back
on a creeper and slides beneath the
undercarriage, one foot sneaking out.
Maintenance is key, he says, and starts
the engine, pulling a rag from his pocket
to wipe down the dipstick and check

the level and colour of fluid.

His hands are stained and scarred,
    look like they would labour all their life
    to love a woman the way they love
    the complicated innards of a car:
    with brains in his fingers, and ears
    that can translate rattle and whine,
    deep knock knock knock under a hood,
    reversing the strange or troublesome
    into something familiar, worth repair.

8

TUNES FOR THE ROAD
NONFICTION
Rachel Barham

I'M SITTING in my Corolla on the top side of Washington, DC, trying to get on the Beltway. I'm driving – if you want to call it that – in the middle of a solid brick of traffic, three lanes of it. It's warm and getting humid, late April, and I've got the windows and the sunroof open. We snail along until I find myself sitting under a sign that says Beltway East: Baltimore.

That's when I remember what's in the CD player and turn it on.

I grew up in Mississippi, a land of blissfully open roads. Seventy miles to the nearest Piggly Wiggly? No problem – see you in an hour. My early driving experiences were ecstatic. In my car, I felt like an eagle in a campaign commercial, soaring free over those Stars and Stripes waving in the background. On a recent visit to my home state, I drove on country roads for five hours and saw one other car.

But DC is a place that vies proudly every year for the title of Traffic Congestion Capital of the United States. LA usually wins, but sometimes we come close. And since martyrdom makes for good conversation at happy hour, we wear that badge proudly. Even more frequently than political rants, these conversations are yelled to co-workers over the earsplitting music that plagues so many of our finer drinking establishments:

"It took me an hour and forty-five minutes to get home from work yesterday!"

"That would be useful information if I had any idea where you live!"

"What?"

Driving in DC, you're less like an eagle and more like an ant, and the cars around you are fellow ants waiting for you to die so they can crawl over your putrefying carcass and get one ant ahead in line.

So here I sit in that ant line. I'm headed out to a gig – I'm a classical singer – and the song on the CD is over before I even arrive at what passes for the open road around here. Once I get on the Beltway, the pace of traffic picks up and I realize I was using my whole brain to drive instead of listening. (This, I admit, is a good thing.) I hit the back button and play it again. Then, settling in, I listen one more time to Bill Staines singing "On a Baltimore mornin' in a January snow." Bill starts the song by setting the scene: he's driving south toward Baltimore just as the winter sun is rising . . .

Did he just rhyme "morn" with "songs"?

I forgive him, as I do every time I hear it.

Damn, I love this song.

Damn. I also love to drive.

The first car that was really mine was a 1982 Mercedes 240D. The D is for diesel. I got it when I was in college and the car was celebrating its quinceañera. But my God, what a car. Matte sky blue, never been wrecked. Hard-top sunroof, after-market CD player, automatic everything, put together with vacuum pods. (Which mostly worked.) Nobody else had a car like it.

On the Natchez Trace between my college in Jackson and my home in Tupelo (birthplace of Elvis!), my bad ass would be rocking to Beethoven symphonies in that Mercedes, which maxed out at about fifty-eight miles per hour. It kept me out of trouble on the Trace – owned by the National Park Service – where the speed limit is a nearly intolerable fifty.

I can smell the interior right now just thinking about it, as comfort-inducing as the scent of my grandmother's pot roast and yeast rolls cooking for Sunday dinner. My father taught me how to change the oil, and to this day I cannot figure out why anyone pays people to do it for them. It's like a conspiracy against women. If you can open a jar of pasta sauce and get into corpse pose in yoga class, you can change the oil in your car. But women don't like to get dirty, they say. Did you ever wipe vomit from the entire contents of the toy box or clean up the raw eggs your husband accidentally smashed in the car trunk? I mean, right, maybe some of us don't *like* it, but at least we're experienced.

With my Mercedes, I learned to reach for the fuse box when something electrical seemed out of whack, instead of whimpering to a mechanic. Replacing windshield wipers and lights, ordering parts on the young but growing Internet to save a couple of dollars: anything I could do myself, I did. German cars were not cheap to fix in Mississippi.

They also weren't common. In practical terms, that meant that diesel fuel was hard to find. Car diesel is the same as truck diesel, but the nozzle for trucks was usually too big for the hole in the Mercedes. So I had to find a place with a diesel pump for cars.

Since nobody used those pumps, the fuel – which has

water in it – could sit there and grow some kind of fungus in it. When that got into my tank and fuel lines, the effect was a gap in the acceleration, as the fuel wasn't getting where it needed to go. I could dance on the accelerator and it had no effect. I found additives that would string it along, but sometimes I'd have to get the whole thing cleaned out professionally.

One of my favorite tricks in this car was fending off tailgaters. If somebody followed me too closely, all I had to do was hit the brake and then the accelerator in quick succession. This would send a plume of black diesel smoke right into the windshield of the offending driver. I don't remember a single case where the driver didn't take the first opportunity to whiz around the slow, stinky Mercedes. With apologies to my fellow air-breathers, mission accomplished.

When I bought the car with money from my savings (more accurately my parents' savings for me), the CD player had a disc in it called *Strictly Trucking*. It was mostly country music, the kind with politics, and it fit nicely with the tastes of the seller. He worked for the American Family Association, a mouthpiece of ultra-conservatism based in Tupelo, where I'd spotted the gem in the Wal-mart parking lot. (Wal-mart had a hyphen in it back then.)

My father and I went for a test drive, and he asked the owner if it was burning any oil. The owner said no. (I guess nobody had ever told him lying was a sin.) After I'd had the car a while, I joked that I never needed to change the oil because it changed itself. Just add new oil, about a quart a month. One less thing on the to-do list!

It felt good to liberate this great car from its previous owner, but in the end, I didn't purge it of its taste in music. It turned out I loved *Strictly Trucking*. I'd be rolling around town or out on the open road, windows and sunroof open, blasting this big-rig music out of my little baby blue sedan.

There's a Big Wheel!
There's a Big Wheel!
He's so much bigger than yeeeeew, There's a Big Wheel!
There's a Big Wheel!

He's so much bigger than meeeee. It's a white gospel ensemble, the kind of thing you'd hear on AM radio on a Sunday morning. The phonemic manipulation with which they manage to rhyme "you" with "me" is a feat that continues to astound me.

Hello. I'm a truck. The deep bass voice criticizes truck drivers and reminds them that they wouldn't exist "if it wasn't for us trucks." This personified 18-wheeler eloquently rhymes the last word with both "nuts" and "luck."

"King of the road," "Truck drivin' man," "Gimme 40 acres and I'll turn this rig around" – I sang along giddily with these most masculine of songs. I either lost or just never looked at the CD case – I was driving, after all – so I didn't know who any of the performers were. I came to love these anonymous voices in all their jeans-wearing, diesel-drunk, entitled glory. Ah, America.

On its fourth alternator, when the whole electrical system got a death sentence, the Mercedes had to go. I was living in DC by then. As much as I longed to keep it around and convert it to a biodiesel, I didn't even have a parking space, much less the time or money for another hobby. I donated it for auction and accidentally left CD 1 of Berlioz's choral-symphonic masterpiece *Te Deum* in the player. But I kept *Strictly Trucking*.

The Bill Staines CD that's in the player now? I got it after I heard "On a Baltimore mornin' in a January snow" on a DC-area radio show called *Traditions* with Mary Cliff ("Folk music and things you can see from there"). Mary introduced it by saying: "Time for a road trip! Here's Bill Staines." I fell in love and bought the CD based on that single hearing.

My current car, the one that replaced the Mercedes, is an aging but intact Corolla that my grandmother helped me buy. I bought it new, this practical, conservative, safe, normal car. I had to order it special because I wanted a stick shift, so I got to choose the color. It had been a long time since I drove stick because my Mercedes was an automatic (the height of luxury when it was born in 1982). I enlisted a friend to coach me so I'd be ready and not strip the thing raw while learning. My first big road trip was to Mississippi so the Corolla and my grandmother could meet.

Before I completed the order for the Corolla, I called my Episcopal priest with one of the only spiritual questions I've ever asked him: "Should I get a red car?" I honestly don't remember his answer, but I think it was along the lines of a noncommittal "if you think that's what would be best." I then called my Aunt Marge with the same question. She said unequivocally that red is safer because people can see it.

So I got a red car – more cherry red than fire-engine red, but still something with enough personality to paper with bumper stickers and make it mine. I tried provocative political stuff for a while, but after the third person flagged me down to ask the meaning of "Misogyny: hard to spell, easy to practice," I decided to concentrate on spreading if not joy then at least not discord. I have some *aloha* on there from Hawaii, but the ones that get the most comments are "Caution: Driver Singing" and "Musicians Duet Better," a gift from my father-in-law.

And that brings us back to the music. I have two music degrees from accredited institutions of higher learning. You can legally call me a Master of Music. I have studied musical rhetoric going back as far as we know music to have existed.

And yet I still cannot explain how the first twenty seconds of "On a Baltimore mornin' in a January snow" – even before a word is sung – can so precisely evoke a big rig barreling down Interstate 95 at seven in the morning. How I can so accurately see through the eyes of its driver, a middle-aged rough-around-the-edges white man who – like me – gets a little tingle deep down at the first glimpse of the quirky Baltimore skyline. How the sound of a few musical instruments can paint a scene of filthy snow, icy now from yesterday afternoon's melt, piled up along the sides of the highway, and the steam coming off it in the first yellow-orange light of morning. The glare of the early sun off the skyscrapers, the possibilities of the coming day, the freedom of the highway, and your sweetheart dozing in the passenger seat.

This is the thing: "On a Baltimore mornin' in a January snow" is not just a good road trip song, it's one of the best love songs in the long and crowded history of love songs. Bill expresses the trouble he had finding the right words to describe his love. He apologizes that finding rhyming words is difficult. (See – I'm glad I forgave him for that rhyme in the first stanza.) He describes his sweetie waking up with a little yawn and what that did to his heart. He professes astonishment at "how such a simple thing as us should ever come to grow." This rhymes, of course, with the title of the song.

I'm the driver in our family. My husband hates driving. (And it's safer for me to drive, since the soothing hum of the engine is more effective than Ambien for him, and he conks out by the time we're three blocks from home.) I do a lot of pondering as I glance at him in the passenger seat, head tilted back, mouth open, twitching in a dream state. How much poetry and music about love has been spilled out over the centuries, and we're no closer to answering Bill's question about "such a simple thing as us."

Like coffee, takeout, and air conditioning, driving is something I know I should give up if I want to be serious about salvaging what's left of the planet (which I do). I don't drive around town if riding my bike is even a remote possibility. I only use the car when I need to: bad weather, hauling stuff, tight connections, and whatnot. Electric cars are better than gas or diesel, but the damn things don't even come in a stick shift.

I guess biking down a hill is kind of like the freedom of a road trip. It's not hard to locate a hill in DC, but finding one without potholes or construction on it is like winning the lottery. On Christmas morning. When I can lift my hands off the handlebars and coast, I come close to that soaring eagle feeling I used to get down South. It's different, though, because biking will never have a soundtrack. Not for me, anyway. I don't think car songs work with bikes, any more than bumper stickers do. It's just a different lifestyle, and one that I'm gradually embracing as I aim for at least a low-car existence.

But I'll always have my memories. As Bill says in his final line – the line that always gets to me the most – "Someday when I'm thinkin' back, again I'll want to go . . ." You know the rhyme by now. Sing along.

Note: "January Snow," words and music by Bill Staines, was originally released on the 1985 album *Wild, Wild Heart* (Philo 1100), but the author's CD is a compilation disc called *Bill Staines: The First Million Miles*, Volume II. *Strictly Trucking* appears to be available still as a print-on-demand CD.

MAKES YOU WONDER
NONFICTION
Marilyn W. Richardson

In 1957, the year I married, few young women owned their own car. So the 1950 Nash Rambler my husband inherited from his father became my car too.

It was dark blue and looked a little like a baby rhinoceros, old-fashioned and boxy. That may have been the reason we decided to buy our own first car—a DKW with a look of its own. To both of us, it seemed a step above the then-popular Volkswagen "Beetle." A little longer with a sleeker look, it was robin-egg blue with a white top. Saving gas was not an issue back then, so the fact that this German-made car would be getting great mileage wasn't a factor in our decision. But because it had a better design than the Bug, we felt smug.

At the time, I didn't wonder at the name DKW. After all, the Germans use abbreviations for many of their cars. BMW—the Bayerische Motoren Werke—for instance. It wasn't until years later that I googled the name and learned that the DKW was called *Das Kleine Wunder* – the little wonder.

In 1958, my husband and I drove our new car to Pennsylvania where Jay would start his work toward a PhD in child and family living at Penn State University and I would eventually earn an MA in theatre arts.

I have few memories of the trip from Utah to Pennsylvania, except for the rolling hills in Iowa and that we stopped in Zanesville, Ohio, and bought dinnerware at an outlet store, black and tan chickens on white. There was plenty of room in the DKW because all we had packed were our clothes and a little bedding.

From there our "little wonder" wheeled us into the southern edge of Pennsylvania. I recall being shocked at the beaten down and grimy look of the houses in the coal mining towns we passed.

State College, however, was unlike those mining towns. Lots of green and a lovely, large campus. Small WWII-era barracks, stair-stepped up a gentle slope, provided housing for grad students. We unloaded our few items into the one-bedroom back half of our new home. Barb and Gil had the other half. No garage for our DKW, of course, but street parking was safe.

We'd arrived, full of excitement, ready to begin this new phase of our lives.

An advantage of living in Center County, PA, home of the Nittany Lions, was that it was possible to drive into New York City two or three times a year to enjoy the sights and sounds of the Big Apple. My bachelor uncle lived in a high-rise near the East River, and he offered us free room and board for those adventurous weekends.

On one of those trips, as our car was being filled at a service station, a man joked, "You need an eyedropper to get the gas in that thing." I was offended. He had no right to make fun of our super special car.

On another, we were on our way back from NYC when the

car broke down in New Jersey. We managed to get to a service station and were sitting on a narrow bench waiting to hear the mechanic's verdict. I felt like we had landed in the middle of nowhere. How would we'd get back to State College if the problem was major? But since Jay remained calm, to a lesser degree, so did I.

A small black-and-white television set, placed up on a shelf so a man behind the counter could watch at eye level, was turned on. A round-faced, bald man, Nikita Khrushchev, who was then First Secretary of the Soviet Union, was shouting hostile and angry words. An interpreter was translating for the American listener.

The owner of the station must have been Russian, because every now and then he would shake his head and say, "That's not what he said." I guessed the translator was softening Khrushchev's words. Probably didn't want to be part of starting WWIII.

The date was October 12, 1960, a Wednesday. A Filipino delegate, Lorenzo Sumulong, speaking to the United Nations General Assembly, had said, ". . . the peoples of Eastern Europe and elsewhere which have been deprived of the free exercise of their civil and political rights and which have been swallowed up, so to speak, by the Soviet Union."

Khrushchev called the man a "jerk," a "stooge," a "lackey," and a "toady of American imperialism," emphasizing his words by banging his shoe on his desk.

To this day, there is controversy over exactly what happened at that meeting: whether he actually used his shoe at all, or it if was because his new shoes were too tight and he'd removed them because his feet hurt, or if he dropped his watch when pounding the table and when he bent to recover it, he saw his shoe and used it – or did he just wave it, or . . .? Because

Khrushchev was a large man, there was some debate as to whether or not he could have retrieved his shoe, as there was limited space for bending. In any case, the pounding and shouting continued with others joining in, until eventually the Assembly President, Frederick Boland, declared the meeting adjourned and slammed his gavel down so hard it broke and the head went flying. British Prime Minister Harold Macmillan quipped, "May we have a translation of that please?"

None of this concerned me as I made it back to State College and focused on my studies as a graduate student in charge of keeping the make-up closet in the theatre department in order, always a mess following a production. My classes were not too challenging, except for lighting design. My favorite was creating short television scripts and serving as director, or sometimes as an actor. Oh, and the class on staging scenes from plays. Ionesco's *Rhinoceros* comes to mind. No one suggested I read up on the playwright or wonder at the symbolism regarding the Nazi invasions of Europe. My only concern was how to create some disturbing sounds—which I think I did successfully by having fellow students kick their heels against the front of the stage and record the noise.

But then came the Cuban Missile Crisis in October 1962, when Kennedy challenged Russia's intention of installing nuclear missiles on an island only ninety miles from Florida. I was sitting in class when the teacher appeared and noted the tension in the classroom—everyone, including me, sat frozen with fear, thinking that the Doomsday Clock must be set at thirty second to midnight. The professor tossed aside his lesson for the day and sat down to talk about the object of our worries. Nuclear annihilation. The end of the world. The end of us. I had great admiration for that teacher and his sensitivity.

At any rate, that is when the famous, "he blinked first" statement was coined, meaning that Khrushchev and Kennedy had a stare down, and Khrushchev backed down. Historians say there was no eyeball to eyeball encounter. Instead, both leaders agreed to give up something. The Russians would dismantle missiles already in place and would turn their ships around and head for home. The U.S. agreed not to invade Cuba again, to dismantle Jupiter MRBNs that had been deployed to Turkey, and to stop nuclear testing.

If we hadn't purchased *Das Kleine Wunder*, if I hadn't an uncle in NYC, if the car hadn't broken down in New Jersey, if the owner of the service station hadn't known Russian, I wouldn't know much about this moment in history and the moments that followed, but now I do.

And if you have read this far, I trust you do, too.

If you are curious as to exactly what our little car looked like, pictures are available online. Remember, it's the baby blue one with a white roof and the sleek, curving lines. And it served us well for many years, in spite of that bit of trouble in New Jersey.

P.S. I have no idea what happened to our two-stroke *Das Kleine Wunder*. Germany stopped building them in 1966, and by that time we had a baby boy and needed a larger car—another phase of our life, other vehicle. There was the white Valiant, repaired by a local mechanic in Brookings, South Dakota, for $7.50. That's right, seven dollars and fifty cents, done more than once. What a deal. But like most people, we got the itch to have something else, and so we purchased a paneled station wagon from brother-in-law Dick (he bought a new car every year, while we kept our cars for eight to ten years), and then the

Honda Civic Hatchback (we did go for smaller cars), and the Toyota Sedan, and finally the Priuses, numbers one and two.

10

ROAD SHOW
POEM

Jessica de Koninck

A GLOWING RED CORVETTE, lights blazing,
    fiberglass shining metallic as a Christmas ornament,
    rolls haltingly down Watchung Avenue, mid-
    point of the funeral cortege.

Part of me has always wanted an arrest-me-red
    car. Maybe not a Vette, maybe a sports sedan, chrome
    deluxe, four Dolby speakers, and most definitely chili
    tomato red. Now I reconsider.

A red car at a funeral, a flame in the center of that
    somber, slow procession, a bright boutonniere
    on a groom's black tuxedo, a bloody wound
    throbbing life in the midst of death.

.   .   .

Better to fade into the crowd. Black suit,
    black hat, black car, slow motion, colorless,
    odorless, indifferent to public acclaim,
    less noticeable than air.

11

YOU ALWAYS REMEMBER YOUR FIRST

NONFICTION

J. Anthony Gohier

MY FIRST CAR was born the same year I was. This was not the first car I drove. That car was haunted—which is another story—and technically that was my mom's car anyway. But the first car I paid my own money for and that had my name on the title was a 1983 Toyota Tercel, a dark tan, boxy, hatchback with just enough rust to make her look cheaper than she really was.

I didn't mind. It was those rust spots that caused the previous driver to give the car back to her mother saying it was hurting her image to drive around campus. Which meant that her mother, who also happened to be my boss, was looking for someone to take a rusty car off her hands for five hundred bucks. Besides, I have a few rust spots myself.

Now I realize she may not sound like much. Typically, you get what you pay for, and most days five hundred dollars just doesn't buy a lot of car, but sometimes it is worth looking past the rust to find out what's under the hood. In Tracy's case (as I eventually named the car) a glance at the odometer was enough to turn my head.

Ninety-thousand miles. She was as old as I and she hadn't even breached the six-digit barrier. This was not a desperate car on her last legs that someone was trying to make a quick buck off. This car had simply been shuffled around for two decades without ever really finding a home. Maybe I could relate.

No, she wasn't perfect. For a start, her speedometer didn't work. Living in Randolph, Utah, I could get away with that for a while, but it only took one ticket coming out of Logan Canyon before I decided it would be cheaper to replace the thing.

I found a used console cluster online and installed it myself. That's not quite as easy as it might sound. Actually installing the cluster was a simple insert Tab-A into Slot-B kind of process, but getting Tracy to open up to that sort of thing meant gently coaxing her out of layers and layers of overlapping dashboard sections, which weren't exactly designed for easy access.

SNL fans may have seen the clip about the Mercury Mistress – the car you can share your most intimate moments with. This was nothing like that. It was more like getting to know someone during a quick change for a dance concert.

Pulling each other's clothes off and throwing new outfits on with nothing more than a few carefully positioned curtains between you and thousands of eager eyes is a good way to get to know someone really well, really fast—especially when you know that in any other setting even suggesting such actions would earn you a slap across the face, at best. There's a kind of trust born in the darkness of stage wings.

That's what I had with Tracy. She and I could trust each other. I took care of her when she wasn't running on all cylinders, and she took care of me when the going got rough. I knew how she handled, and I knew which noises meant she needed a little extra T-L-C. And I fully believe I would still be driving her today if it weren't for the deer.

I was rounding a corner on I-80, headed back to school after pulling a forty-hour weekend shift at a youth ranch academy. The facility had staff beds on site, so I wasn't driving drowsily, but it was nearing midnight on Sunday and I had an oral exam in French Monday morning, so I was cruising at a comfortable 75 mph, which I thought was the speed limit, though my brother was surprised I didn't get a ticket when I told that to the cop the next day.

Einstein said time is relative, and I'm inclined to agree with him because the moment the deer appeared in my headlights was a fraction of a second and an eternity all at once. Then the moment was over and everything went dark. I felt myself come to a stop, then took a few moments to make sure I was still breathing.

My trembling hand found the door latch and I stepped out into the autumn night. Passing cars threw splashes of light across me in a kind of slow-motion strobe-light effect as I surveyed the scene. There was no sign of the deer other than what it had done to Tracy, whose front end now resembled an accordion.

Later, riding in the back of my brother's car, I realized what those accordion wrinkles meant. When my brother's car went off the road he ended up in a neck brace for a week. But, as I examined Tracy's corpse, the thought never crossed my mind to worry about what might have happened to me. She was too old to have modern safety features like airbags, but when push came to shove she didn't need them. She just took it all, like a champion. I walked away, but Tracy never drove again.

Sure, I loved my first car, but she loved me too. At least I'm pretty sure that's what the Bible calls it. So when I say I'm looking for a car I can trust, that's what I'm talking about. The new models might be prettier or have flashier toys, but can I trust them to take care of my kids? And if it means knowing that my car will be there when I need it, and will do what it takes to make sure life goes on even after running head-on into a couple hundred pounds of wildlife, then I can overlook a few rust spots.

NOT QUITE FLUENT: MY ONGOING EFFORTS TO MASTER AUTOMOBILE LANGUAGE AND CULTURE

NONFICTION

Felicia Rose

IN MY EARLY twenties I landed a job teaching English to refugees recently arrived in New York. One woman, Asya, had been a student at the University of Tehran. Three weeks into the course, she exchanged her loose black robe for tight black jeans. "I hope to attend university here in the spring," she said. Given her progress with English, I had no doubt she would.

Her father, Mehdi, also in my class, showed far less promise. "Aye ham ebuk," he would say. ("No, Baba," Asya would mouth, "I have a book.") His plastic sandals and unkempt salt-and-pepper beard brought to mind someone who sold aluminum pans from a pushcart. How he functioned in Manhattan is anyone's guess.

Whenever I reflect on my efforts to assimilate into car culture, I think about Mehdi. More to the point, I am Mehdi.

A refugee from New York City, I now live in a small town in the Intermountain West where nearly everyone fifteen and over drives. When I first arrived, my impulse was to walk. That's what New Yorkers do, walk: to and from the library, across the Williamsburg Bridge, around Fort Tryon Park. Even those who own cars often walk. Why? It's less claustrophobic than the subway, more convenient than the bus. Certainly, it's quicker than driving, especially on occasions when one turns down a one-way street only to find a piano plunked in the middle while the moving men have gone to get lunch.

Then there's the issue of street parking. An advanced version of musical chairs, it contains too few spots for vehicles. And on alternate-side parking times, half of those spots must remain vacant for the street-sweeping truck that may or may not come along to clean them.

A friend of mine from India, already trilingual when he arrived in the city, decided to learn Spanish to help him pass the time while he searched for a place to park. Now, after several years of daily quests that can last upward of half an hour, he enjoys a working command of the language.

On assorted holidays, the city suspends alternate-side parking, which means car owners do not need to move their vehicles. Said friend has expressed gratitude for the city's holiday schedule not only because it saves him the hassle of finding another parking spot, but also because it's a reminder to him, a secular chap, to wish his parents a happy Diwali.

Alternate-side parking has fashioned particular cultures around the city. Though technically illegal to double-park, car owners, many of whom use their vehicles only to leave the city, but not for daily commutes, have little choice but to drive around in search of that rare spot or else double-park. So as not to prevent vehicles parked near the curb from being able to move, these folk have developed a system of placing their address and phone number on the dashboard. In this way, if someone's car is blocked by a double-parked car, they can contact the owner to move their car. Several times a month, the man who lived next door to me would run out of his apartment blotting shaving cream off his face in a mad dash to move his car.

Speaking of parking spots, the Flatiron District Home Depot lacks them. As a result, it's not unusual to see people exit the store with a slab of drywall atop their head or a rubber plunger tucked into an armpit. Of course, one can hail a taxi. But why deny oneself the pleasures of walking? I've been known to carry brooms and buckets along Broadway.

Not long after moving to Utah, I attempted similar feats. On one occasion, intent on reviving a garden bed while my wife, Monte, and her car were at work, I walked a mile to the hardware store to buy a bag of manure. On my way home, no fewer than three drivers offered me a lift. I declined out of concern for their cars. (Though composted, the manure smelled as if a cow had excreted it that morning.) Self-conscious about carrying a forty-pound bag of fertilizer along Main Street, I imagined myself an unassimilated Mehdi. Still, this particular experience did not convince me to hone my driving skills or purchase a car.

Nor did the countless times I lugged canvas bags of groceries home in downpours and snowstorms. Or those occasions I had to wait for the weekend to buy chicken feed or hay for our homestead. (From time to time I'd fantasize about conveying bales of straw on the city bus or else procuring a couple of draft horses to pull these items home in a cart.)

Why this resistance to owning and driving a car? Here are some of the stock answers I offered: I didn't want to add gas-guzzling metal to our ecologically-challenged locale. I didn't want to spend money on a vehicle. I didn't want to become sedentary.

Much as Mehdi could have trimmed his beard or bought an updated pair of pants at the thrift store, I could have exerted more of an initial effort to assimilate into the culture in which I now lived. But walking was familiar and pleasant. I liked – and still like – the satisfaction of a robust walk: the way it contributes to physical exuberance, clarity of thought, and serenity of spirit.

I also liked identifying as a walker.

Not a driver. This though I got my license at the age of twenty, a month after graduating from college. I passed the driving test on my first try. On a stick shift. After a mere three weeks of practice. Sans driver's ed. These details became a badge of honor.

The only glitch, a minor technical one, was that except for along the deserted stretch of South Brooklyn road where I took the exam, I really couldn't drive. I'd simply learned the rules: put the car into first gear when driving between one and fifteen miles an hour, second gear for sixteen to thirty, and so forth (of course, there never was a so forth). But I lacked the experience required to transform that knowledge into muscle memory.

Until the pistachio-nut incident spurred me to change.

Monte and I had been snacking on them when she turned ashen and began to throw up. For two or three seconds her breathing became strained. It was during those two or three seconds when I imagined I might need to take her to the hospital that I felt for the first time the urgency to drive.

Which I proceeded to learn how to do. Not as someone who dabbles in French until she can parrot textbook conversation. But rather as one who immerses herself in the language until it rolls off her tongue.

But first I needed to review basic grammar.

I began the next morning by sitting in the driver's seat. And then learning how to adjust it so I could reach the pedals and see over the dash. After a few more refreshers involving side-view mirrors, rear-view mirror, blinkers, wipers, ignition, and lights, I depressed the brake, put the gear in drive, and then bore down on the gas pedal until the speedometer needle reached five. Now we were moving.

Recuperated from her allergic reaction, Monte sat in the passenger seat fiddling with a bunch of CDs. "Classical or Jazz?" she asked.

Here I was operating a potentially lethal machine, and it mattered whether we listened to Scarlatti or Coltrane? Poor dewy-eyed Monte. Clearly, I'd need to fret for us both.

Even so, my driving became news. My father-in-law, a Wyoming native known to drive along icy hairpin roads with the nonchalance of an ambler through grasslands, wondered if I'd succeeded in outpacing the bicyclists. A beloved aunt, who a few years earlier had threatened to buckle me into her grandson's rear-facing car seat if I didn't refrain from gasping each time she pressed on the gas, waxed hopeful when she heard about my endeavor. "Maybe now that you spend time in the driver's seat," she said, "You'll not be so anxious."

Maybe, I thought, though highly unlikely.

Still, I began making forays – hardware store, supermarket, post office – much as fledgling birds do from the nest. Then one day I drove myself to the diner for lunch. What independence I felt pulling into the parking lot, carrying the car key, ordering a burger and fries.

It didn't take long before I was wending through canyons in search of places to hike. This rugged backcountry with its craggy mountains, glacial lakes, and riparian trails edged with juniper and pine spoke to my need for natural beauty. As well, I discovered, it proved nonpareil for the robust walking I loved.

"I think I'd like to get my own car," I announced to Monte.

"Why don't we continue to share the one we have?"

"No," I said with such force I surprised even myself. Impelling that response was the desire to take myself to a greasy spoon or on a hike whenever the spirit moved me. And haul firewood or scrap metal besides. (Clearly, I was becoming a rustic, which involved acculturating into rural ways.)

Some months later, we learned about a 2007 Subaru Outback for sale. For all I knew, the owner might have been hawking a 2007 Matchbox. But everyone who did know, and that everyone meant Monte, considered it an excellent choice. So I bought it.

Beyond the proverbial VW Beetle with flowers, aka hippie car, I had no clue what motor vehicles expressed about their owners. I could no more distinguish between a Corolla and Corvair, let alone apply any sort of semiotic analysis, than the average Intermountain Westerner could deconstruct the socio-economic distinctions between a Classic Six and a Floor Through.

So it came as a surprise when I learned that massive pickup trucks hinted at overcompensation by the apparently diminutive men who drove them. (What they say about female driver-owners I still don't know.)

Another bolt from the blue, and one less auspicious for me, was that the car I now owned and had been driving for nearly a year apparently signified 'lesbian.' (I've since come to know it may also imply 'outdoorsy type,' 'health-care professional,' or 'teacher,' but apparently 'lesbian' is the first connotation.) Why had no one told me *before* I bought the car? "I thought you knew," was the standard response.

Now that I did know, I felt as if I'd been wearing a tee shirt with what I assumed was an abstract design, but which actually read, 'Goji berries are delicious' in Chinese. Yes, I like goji berries, but I'd prefer not to have my quirky character reduced to that single trait. Is there no car that communicates a medley of qualities, let's say, 'grammarian, gardener, and goji-berry groupie'? Or one that insinuates an Existentialist flair: "Mutable mystery even to myself"?

Still, I've come to appreciate my Subaru over these past five years. Reluctant though I am to reduce myself (or anyone else) to a typecast, I admit to valuing the unembellished versatility of the machine. I'm thinking now of the times we've used it to haul fruit trees and shrubs; the snowy stints though canyons for midwinter hikes; the evening our camping tent blew down in a windstorm, and so we lowered the backseat, laid out our sleeping bags, and enjoyed a decent night's rest.

Though increasingly fluent in operating the machine, I remain ignorant about maintenance. My understanding of what takes place under the chassis amounts to zero. Equal is my proficiency at adding windshield-wiper fluid or checking the oil. With regard to the latter, I'm quite sure it involves a clean white rag and a thin metal stick. Beyond that I'm clueless.

Apparently that's not a secret. The last time I had an appointment for an oil change, the automotive shop was bustling. In order to save time, the mechanic asked the two drivers ahead of me to pop their hoods. Within seconds, the fronts of their cars opened like roaring mouths of beasts. When the mechanic approached my car, she made the same request. But then she looked more closely at the driver. "Never mind," she said. "I'll take care of it."

Sitting in the waiting room of the shop, I wondered about Asya and Mehdi. No doubt, Asya had graduated from university. Maybe she'd even attended graduate school and was now teaching linguistics. As for Mehdi, I have a hard time picturing him a student of Tannen or Pinker. Still, I imagine that by now he can not only say "I have a book," but can read one as well.

As for myself, when the mechanic announced that my car was ready, I asked her about changing the transmission fluid. She proceeded to explain the mechanics of gears, axles, and driveshafts. I could see that the topic animated her, and so I listened and nodded. In truth, I understood little.

Afterward, I found solace in my car, where I chose a CD, slid it into the stereo, and then headed to the green-waste facility to buy a carload of mulch for our garden.

13

I WANT TO ASK YOU
POEM
Jessica de Koninck

Do they ride motorcycles in heaven?
like the Suzuki you drove to Cape Cod to meet me
after midnight, or the BMW you rode with your brother
from France to Egypt, then from Nevada to California to bury
your father, or the one you saw crash and the rider quivered
on the car hood where he'd landed, and you did not ride
after that? Your bike remains in the garage.
I have not moved it.

Maybe you get a new Harley in heaven. Doesn't need gas.
Never breaks down. Easy Rider, I hope you chose a Ducati,
your favorite, something with class, expensive, or an Indian,
sleek and speedy, with deco letters, the kind they don't make
anymore. Perhaps it has a Cupid face and heart-shaped
fenders like the Valentine you drew for me.
I kept that too.

Better than wings I think, a two stroke, or a four stroke, faster,

more comfortable, more maneuverable. You can park it
outside. Wings would be clumsy, weigh you down.
Not like a bike. Your helmet, your saddlebags,
your black leather jacket, I kept everything.
You still flew away.

14

SOAP BOX DERBY

FICTION

Stephen Page

JONATHAN WAS WEARING his blue Cub Scout uniform and carrying a three-inch square, nine-inch long block of wood in his hand. The block swung with each stride he made. He was walking south on John R Road and came to the corner of 11 Mile Road, where he stopped because the streetlight was green. Telway Burgers was across the street on the east side of John R, and Jonathan had two quarters in his pocket, enough to buy a burger, an order of fries, and a coke. He was hungry, but he wanted to get home just as soon as he could in order to start carving the wood into the shape of a race car for the soap box derby event that would take place the following week. He paced back and forth on the cracked, crumbling sidewalk, waiting for the light to change. He ran his fingertips lightly over the badges above his left-breast pocket, and then over the Madison Heights Troop 9 bear-cub patch on his right sleeve. He tightened and then loosened the yellow scarf around his neck. The light changed to green and he ran as fast as he could across 11 Mile. He kept running for one block on John R, then turned right on

Cowan Avenue, kept running till he reached Alger Avenue, and swung left. He ran to the fourth house on the left, cut across the lawn, and leapt over the three porch steps to the top, teetered there for a second, ripped open the aluminum front door with the big B on it, and fell on the living-room carpet, panting and soaked with sweat.

His mother, who ran her own nail-salon business inside the laundry room, was approaching the living room. He could hear her Dr. Scholls clomping on the kitchen tiles. "Don't slam the door," she shouted, "ever again!" Then in a softer, sweeter tone, more like the elegantly-tanned model actress that she was, said, "You disturb my customers, honey. And you can break the aluminum. Or rip the screen. That costs a lot of money."

"I . . ." he panted, "I . . ."

"Yes? Sweetie," she knelt down and put her hand on his soaked head. "Tell me. Are you all right? Did something happen?"

"I have to—" He held up the block of wood. "I have to carve a race car out of this wood with my Cub Scout knife for the Soap Box Derby event. It happens next week."

"Don't worry, honey. Dad will help you. Wait 'til he gets home from work. Now take off that wet uniform, go take a bath, and by that time, Dad will be home and we can talk over dinner. Go. Go, now. Go. Get up, slowly. I have to get back to my customers. Love you honey." She kissed the back of his neck.

Jonathan cradled the block of wood, went to his room, and flopped on his bed. He removed his Cub Scout cap from his head, and rubbed his crew cut. He looked out the window and studied the crab apple tree in his backyard, the same tree he had climbed so many times. The leaves were dull green in the afternoon sun, and the inedible fruit hung in dark red clusters. He wondered why someone would even plant a tree that grew inedible fruit, but when he saw a robin fly out of it, he thought that there might be meaning in everything. He rose from the bed and walked down the hallway to the bathroom to take a shower.

He waited on the floor of the living room in his denim shorts and paisley short-sleeve shirt with the piece of wood in one hand and his Cub Scout pocketknife in the other. When he heard his father's footsteps on the porch, he shuddered. How many times had he wished he would not hear his father's footsteps? How many times had he wished his father dead? He felt immediately guilty for his thoughts, and the anticipation returned—the want of creating, the want to win the soap-box derby, the need of fatherly guidance and instruction, the need of a fatherly rub on the head, the need of a simply spoken: "Hey, Son. How are you?"

His father appeared in the frame of the front screen door. When Jonathan saw the scowl on his father's face, he nervously tried to slice a chunk out of the wood with his pocketknife, but the wood would not yield to the dull blade.

His father entered in his greasy blue uniform with the UAW patch over the left breast pocket, stepped heavily into the house, glancing at what his son was doing as he walked by him, tracking grease and metal shavings through the carpet, then flopped down on the sofa, turning his back to his son. He mumbled, "What are you doing with a knife? Put it away. God! You're so damn weird." He kicked off his black shoes, revealing heavy white socks. The smell of bad cheese filled the living room. Jonathan started to tell him about the derby, started to ask him for his help, only stuttered out the word "I," but his father was already snoring.

Jonathan stood and stared at his father's back, listened to his snore, and clutched the knife tightly in his right hand. He loosened his grip on the knife and flipped it around in his hand a few times. He gripped it again and got down in a crouching position. He straightened his spine and using his thumb, closed the pocketknife with a 'snap'. He slumped his shoulders, looked down at his Converse All Stars, and trudged to his room, the block of wood in one hand, the useless knife in the other.

THE OL' GOAT
NONFICTION

Janine Harrison

I WAS ABOUT to hop into the driver's seat of the '67 Pontiac GTO when a man from another pump asked, "Is that your dad's car?" He smiled.

"It was," I answered. "He died last week."

His smile ceased and face grayed. "I...I'm sorry—"

I barely nodded, got into the car, and pulled away.

———

The only time I saw a doctor when I was a kid was for required immunization shots. We didn't have health insurance. But once, when I was still quite small, I ran a fever that worried my mom enough that Dad drove us to Dr. Kratz's office, two streets south. Mom, you see, didn't drive.

We left through the front door. Sunlight peeped through our two maple trees in the parkway. Dad usually drove an orange, long-bed Ford pick-up. A carpenter, he had black toolboxes attached to each side of the bed and an aluminum ladder secured to a frame on top. But I heard acceleration and turned my head to see him pulling up in a vehicle I'd never seen – a midnight-purple car with no roof! We got in and Mom held me on her lap. I smiled widely the whole two blocks as the breeze stroked my hot forehead, blonde, Brady Bunch hair blowing backward.

———

The Pontiac hardly ever left the garage. Just after I turned sixteen, when the ol' man died, it had 47,000 original miles on it. When it was driven, though, it was always an adventure.

My dad was forty-four when I was born, so he was an older father, but only biologically. Every once in a while, he and I would be in the car alone and stopped at a light next to a young whippersnapper in a hotrod, revving his engine. When this happened, Dad's right hand would remove the chrome cover from the dual gate and move the shifter into the slot.

(Under the hood, the GTO had a 400 engine.)

When the light turned green, Dad would quietly and steadily accelerate, blowing the young'n's car away. He'd never say a word, but after, a small smile would creep onto his face.

———

We didn't have much, and I was used to our stuff being old and, therefore, bad.

Dad rarely had a reason to pick me up from school. When he did, it was usually in the truck and since he always piled a bunch of tools against the passenger side door, I'd have to climb in through the driver's seat and sit close to him. (It was embarrassing.)

One time, though, he didn't just pull up *to* the school – he flew around the corner and pulled onto the playground in the GTO to pick me up. Two boys, Terry and Matt (I had a crush on Terry) said, "That's your dad's car? It's so cool!"

———

Perhaps the 4th of July before he died, Dad took the car out of the garage early one morning and, in the alley, washed it, then Turtle Waxed it (the white kind that came in a jar with a sponge stored in the lid that you rubbed on in circles. I once tried this later, myself, left the wax on too long, and had a devil of a time getting it back off! This was a rare occurrence, indeed. *What's up?* I wondered.

When finished, he took a bath, got ready, and drove off. He and the Goat, plus three passengers, all in official regalia, including caps, represented the VFW in the Dolton parade. I saw photos given to Dad later on.

———

Dad was an alcoholic. By the end, he would self-medicate the cancer writhing throughout his body with a case of beer a day.

He occasionally took cans of Stroh's or Old Style with him in the truck. He'd stow beer on the dashboard as he sat in the driver's seat.

Mom and I mostly remained at home. Dad frequently drank at a bar, Pete's Lone Oak on Halsted Street, stopping in on his way home from a day of building garages or doing interior remodeling jobs. Every once in a while, though, we went to a party together, in which case he pulled the Goat out of the garage. I used to think it was funny when we'd drive home afterward and he kept missing the front door lock when aiming the house key, and I'd have to take his keys from him to do it myself.

Only once do I remember him driving the GTO drunk during the daytime.

I don't know why we were in the car. Maybe it was left out from the night before?

Dad and I always drove to Village Liquor together. It had always been our thing. He'd get his beer, and we'd approach the counter and for years an old cashierwould tease, "Is that your grandfather?"

I'd scowl. "No, that's my dad!"

Then the cashier would wink and hand me a five-cent pretzel on the house.

By now, I was a teenager, but I still sometimes went along for the ride.

I think I went along that day because I knew he was drunk and was worried. I think my mom tried to protest (something rare), but I overruled her. She didn't have much agency, and I was willful.

Usually, Dad and I took School Street to and from the store. We had to go over a bridge that bypassed train tracks. This time, after he made his purchase, Dad took the long way – 138th all the way to Halsted Street and turned left to go over that bridge instead. It was a larger bridge – one with a cement divider between the four lanes.

Dad turned too soon and entered the left side of the divider.

I didn't realize it right away. I wasn't old enough to drive, and I didn't pay that close of attention to the road. Yet, something seemed off. When we made it to the top, I could clearly see that we were on the wrong side, since the traffic below faced up at us.

We didn't wear seatbelts back then. It never even occurred to me to buckle mine. Instead, I planted my feet on the dashboard to brace for impact and stated, "We're gonna die."

Dad looked at me for a second, as if sizing me up. Then, he descended the bridge until we made it just beyond the guard rail to our left. Hopping a curb, he took the Goat into a field, where he simply cut the corner between Halsted and the intersecting street. Once the car was back on pavement, he tilted back his head and laughed.

Years later, my creative-writing professor Charlie Tinkham, who was about the same age as Dad, would listen to me read about this ordeal and say, "Your father was a sick man."

I would find it vindicating.

———

In Illinois, we had driver's education in high school, but parents were expected to take their teenagers out for additional practice. I couldn't learn on the truck because it was a three-speed stick, so Dad had no choice but to take me out in his precious ragtop.

He took me to the VFW hall parking lot on 138th Street. We switched seats.

He gave me a few pointers and had me practice turns in the lot for a few minutes before having me make a right onto the street. We wound through our neighboring town, Dolton, on fairly busy roads until we reached Sibley Boulevard, where he told me to turn right, back toward home.

I had to go over a bridge driving his behemoth '67 car in 1984.

It wasn't just any bridge.

It was a bridge under construction, half shorn away with one lane in each direction, barriers on both sides.

I was terrified, and I doubt that I breathed during the entire up, over, and down, as I concentrated on keeping the car steady and straight, and not scraping its sides on cement.

I made it! *Whew.*

Talk about throwing the child into the deep end of the pool and yelling, "Now, swim!"

(But, it *did* give me confidence.)

We're almost home. Thank God!

When we entered our block, Eggleston Avenue, I heard Dad say, "Move to your left."

It was a typical residential street, with no traffic coming. But I didn't realize that under those conditions, you could drive straight down the middle. I wanted to stay to the right, like a good girl. So, when Dad said, "Move to your left," my brain heard, "Move to your right."

Dad yelled, "More to the left!"

Again, I moved the Goat closer to the parked cars on my right, dangerously close to drivers' side mirrors.

Finally, Dad pointed left. "That way, Janine!"

We lived only five houses into the block, so I soon parked the car, unscathed.

Dad exited. His year-round tan face was gray.

———

For my sixteenth birthday, Dad fixed up my much older sister's 1969 VW Beetle. By "fixed up," I mean that he welded sheet metal to the floor pan, so that I couldn't see the ground below me as I drove. (Just don't ask about the gap between the driver's door and floor. Or that I would have to scrape the inside of the windshield in the winter before I drove, because there was no front defrost.) We hosted a sleepover, inviting my dearest friends. They gave me my first mini-skirt. Mom bought me an ice-cream cake in my favorite color, mint green, decorated like a tennis ball (I was on the high school team). And, Mom and Dad took my friends and me out front and introduced me to my new car – a black "pregnant rollerskate" with red vinyl interior! Best. Birthday. Ever!

———

Dad knew he was dying. He had his brother-in-law Gene take him to a V.A. hospital for lung X-rays without telling us. We'd find them stored in a high-boy dresser drawer after he passed. It was no surprise: he'd been in Nagasaki to help with clean-up as a soldier after the bomb was dropped, he'd worked in asbestos-filled buildings for decades, and he'd smoked two packs of Pall Mall unfiltered cigarettes a day. He quit smoking toward the end but that was closing the barn door after every animal had escaped.

I came home from a friend's sleepover on one Sunday in September and sat down at the kitchen table. Dad was reading the newspaper, and Mom was hand-washing the dishes. I started blabbering away about my fun night when Dad looked up at me from his paper. "Mom – Dad's eyes are yellow."

"Oh, Bob – let me see!"

Three days later, in the same V.A. hospital, he died.

———

I didn't cry at Dad's funeral. I would later learn that detail had spread quickly around my circle of friends.

What I couldn't know then is that I grieve deeply, and it takes a long time for it to rise to the surface. I was still numb at the service.

That summer, I'd fallen in love for the first time, and I'd just entered my junior year and been accepted to the premiere dance team, T-Ettes. Dad had been heavy. Within the last three years, he'd disowned my older brother, thrown me headfirst into a kitchen wall, and hit me so hard on the side of the head that I'd nearly passed out, a black checkerboard of dots appearing before my eyes. My grades had suffered, and I'd even become anorexic for a while.

With him gone, I was determined to be perfect – student, girlfriend, dancer, friend, and daughter. I tried to take over for my dad as the "man" of the family and to grow up overnight.

I succeeded!

For about five months.

Then I crashed and burned and burned and burned for years. But that, as they say, is another essay.

At first, I drove the Bug.

(I also drove Dad's truck around the block once when Mom wasn't home, just to prove to myself that I could do it. Then we sold it.)

I don't remember when or why I first started taking the GTO out of the garage, but I know that I did so at least twice that fall. Once, I volunteered for it to be in a parade, representing the T-Ettes. I drove, the adult leader beside me, while the rest of the girls danced behind it as we steered the parade route.

The second time, I picked up a couple of friends, and we

headed to school for an evening basketball game. It was raining and the roads were slick. A drunk pulled out of a liquor store lot on Halsted Street and never sped up. I couldn't switch lanes because a car was beside me, so I applied the brakes hard and began to fishtail. Next thing I knew, the car did a 360 and the rear, right quarter panel ended up smashing a fire hydrant.

I cried. I knew Dad was a rolling beer can in his grave.

I guess the tires were bald. That was the thing – Mom and I didn't know diddly about car maintenance, which would later prove the Pontiac's downfall.

But not before summer, summer, summer!

———

By the following summer, I'd plummeted into depression and self-destructed, losing the good thing I had with my first love in the process. But summer makes everything better, right? Especially when you inherited a convertible!

I lived the farthest north of my friends from the places we liked to hang out, and I was the only one who owned a car, so naturally, I drove.

Dad had built our two-story, two-car garage with an attached patio. It had separate overhead doors for each stall and abutted an alley.

The GTO *barely* fit in the garage and to pull down the door behind it, it had to be nudged with quick, light taps to the gas within a few inches of the wooden stairway. Getting the car in and out, in fact, required an approach that, due to neighbors' fences on the other side of the alley, could only be made from one direction and involved an outward swing, followed by several back and forth movements, and three-point turnaround style, just to face the stall door.

The car was so important to me that I never once scraped a side while entering the narrow space or bumped the stairs ahead.

I loved the GTO – its wood and chrome dash and console. Its black leather seats. (A boyfriend I would soon meet would teach me to Armor-All them, and they'd be so shiny and slick that sometimes passengers or I would slide down farther than expected when sitting and if there was a sudden stop, well...)

I can't recall when the alley was finally paved, but I can still hear the sounds of the GTO: the initial, quick awakening growl of the engine when I turned the key in the ignition; the sharp click, switching gear from "P" to "R"; the purr as I gently coaxed her out of the garage; the meeting of rubber on gravel – the crunch-grind as I turned the wheel. Then I'd stop, shift her back into park, undo the latches on each side where the wind-shield met the top, and the mechanical whirring as the car "ceiling" opened to the beautiful sky and the black top slowly nestled itself into storage behind the back seat.

One by one, I'd pick up my crew of girl friends. No one used the doors. Everyone jumped over the side a la *Happy Days*.

It was the 80s, so having teen-girl hair in a convertible meant one of two things: 1. Ponytail, or 2. Enough Final Net hairspray on hair feathered all the way around for us to have created our own personal hole in the ozone layer. (Sorry, Mother Earth! We didn't know!)

Then, we'd go scope out guys. We'd drive through Friar Tuck's video arcade parking lot. We'd make an early evening stop at Wright's Barnyard, a family entertainment center with not only an arcade but also go-karts, mini-golf, and batting cages. Once dusk became dark, we'd head to the trifecta of hangout spots: White Castle, Rocky Rococo, and Venture parking lots, adjoined. While this may sound anticlimactic, our sheer number is what mattered! We who invaded West Beach during the day, backing traffic up all the way onto 80/94 were of such magnitude that before the end of the summer, the Calumet City police would hand out tickets for loitering in an effort to discourage us. (P.S. It didn't work.)

We were high on life –before we ever started drinking alcohol – and sometimes as we cruised the White Castles square, strange guys would jump into the car and ask to drive it! We flirted and joked with boys until parental curfews pulled us back home like a retracting leash. Once, I was chasing a friend's brother's truck through the Venture lot and didn't see a cement island. "Janine, stop!" yelled the friend. I slowed just in time to get the GTO stuck on top. Guys pushed us back off.Red faced, I called Mom and told her that I was spending the night at my friend's house – nothing more, and her brother spent most of the next day welding the exhaust system bracket, so it wouldn't drag.

Sigh...

———

Within the next couple of years, lack of oil changes would lead to black smoke billowing from the exhaust – a rod knock. Another friend's brother would swap out the ruined engine for one that ran. My much older brother, always helpful after the fact, would criticize, "You should'n'a done that – now the serial numbers don't match!"

Looking at the car made me sad by then – sad that I'd hurt Dad's prized possession. I'd also become sad about Dad.

With my approval, Mom would sell her to a neighbor for $5,000 to help pay for my college education.

If I had it to do over, I'd take a semester or two off of college, earn the money, and keep the GTO.

————

I'm fifty-one now and I still miss the ol' Goat.

16

SAUDADE OFF EXIT 32
POEM
Kamal E. Kimball

A MILE OUT OF LEBANON, Ohio
   all the Ryder trucks long haul the length of 71.
   They could be my father in his 18-wheeler,
   flushed with pride at the shine on his rig,
   and fresh from the menthol dip
   tucked in his lip like all the shit
   he doesn't say. But it's been 10 years
   since he slid the keys over the desk
   when the doc said his spine is rebar
   that'll never get unbent,
   and I'm just headed home.
   B105 for company and Johnny calls in,
   says he wants to wish all the girls
   in Campbell County goodnight.
   Think of all those girls,
   the clean, sweet smell when they lay
   down their heads and their hair
   is golden hay and warm as the last sip

of Coors. And there's Johnny, cranking
his radio, trying to wring out
all the longing a country song's got.
He doesn't know but the word
for this pang, the word he wants,
is Portuguese. I think of calling in
to tell him *saudade*. He is
and I am, in a parking lot, alone.
Bright stabs of tail light and the weigh
-station man in his neon vest is a father.
And the fathers in baseball caps,
dashboard light on their faces,
are stopping on their way home
to the girls in their beds, girls dreaming
of a Johnny someday, a man
who says he's thinking of them
when they sing themselves goodnight.

This poem first appeared in *One* by Jacar Press, Issue 14
(http://one.jacarpress.com/issue-14/#Kamal%20E.%20Kimball)

17

THE WHEELS ON
THE BUS
NONFICTION

Patricia DiMaio

TURNS out the wheels on the bus do go round and round, even after all the children in all the schools have graduated and moved on. My father always had an active project and for the longest time, his project was keeping my mother alive, rotating the family's time between New York City and Miami, ever chasing an elusive spot on what was, at the time, the rare dialysis machine. But the miracle of organ transplant brought that project to a joyous conclusion and, in 1969, it was time for my father to find a new project, hopefully a little less tinged with blood and the specter of death.

And just like that, he procured a big old 1969, yellow school bus. It had a manual transmission, no power steering, and no power brakes. On the streets of the five boroughs of New York City, it seemed as though it had no shocks either.

He enlisted his crew of mechanically adept friends to convert this monstrosity from a student conveyance to a supremely non-posh camping conveyance. There was the electrician friend and the plumber friend and the architect friend.

Pops had a large enclosed space available in his big auto repair, body work, auto parts business in Richmond Hill, so he could work through the winter. It was an added bonus for us kids that the architect was my uncle, so when 'the bus' (as it rather boringly came to be known) was ready to hit the road, we set out with four adults and six children for the maiden voyage to somewhere in upstate New York.

What about an interior decorator friend? Well, there really was none with any formal credentials, with the result that there was never any formal theme for the interior. As an adult, I prefer to think it was postmodern, because form did in fact follow function—like a bloodhound, with an absolute absence of frivolous ornamentation. Frugality was the watchword. Mom mainly confined her decorating activities to deciding on curtain patterns and Naugahyde colors. The dinette area (which converted to a sleeping platform, of course) was a solid dark beige and the back bunk area was an indescribable green. Two-thirds of the top bunk folded down to make a seating area for the wee ones. Given the seeming inability of the bus's shock absorbers to absorb even the mildest of road crater-induced jolts, we kids played a game of 'try to stay seated as we hit pothole after pothole.' Getting bounced to the floor was fairly amusing initially, but if one wanted to actually sleep during a long trip, one needed a plan. Just start out on the floor and save yourself the trouble and the bruising. A dubious bonus of the minimal suspension system? We always knew when we had crossed over from Westchester County to the Bronx on a journey home. The roads deteriorated quickly and with a vengeance. And, honestly, our mutt canine, Tiger, didn't enjoy the lack of suspension or roar of the engine either. For all his bravado at home, chasing cats and escaping from the house for overnight benders, he was a pathetic, panting, quaking wreck the whole time the bus was in motion. And if we had to stop short? The poor guy's nails did nothing to stop him from sliding along the linoleum until he was halted by slamming into the back of the passenger chair or into the nether region under the dashboard.

A typical camping weekend started on Friday afternoon with the families assembled, dining on New Park Pizza takeout. The bus had been provisioned and all the hatches had been battened down, because a rough ride was always expected. It was not a rare occurrence for a cabinet door to come unhinged on a sharp turn and rain its contents down on the counter and floor. As a result, drinking out of a real glass or eating off a real plate did not happen on the road.

Now how did six children, all pre-teens, manage to stay busy on a multi-hour voyage to upstate New York the New Jersey shore or rural Connecticut? Employing the rules of the elementary school class trip, the back of the bus was cool and sitting up front with the parents was lame. With my fave cousin and me being the eldest (say, eleven or twelve), we didn't care what the little ones did, as long as they stayed out of our way. And, the very youngest cousin did often take refuge in the front, hunkering down with her mom as pops and my uncle shared the driving, often managing to switch drivers while the bus remained in motion...midstream, much to my amazement then and to this day.

We grew up in the days following the dawning of the Age of Aquarius. We older children devised a survey that incorporated a sign of the times. And that sign was the v-shaped, two-fingers-up peace sign. Out the back door window, formerly the school bus's emergency hatch, we flashed the peace sign at other vehicles on the road. We flashed that sign with abandon and zeal. And with pad and pencils in hand, we kept a tally of which cars returned the peace sign, by state. I recall a few obscene gestures returned our way, but most vehicle drivers and passengers either flashed the 'v' or just ignored us.

So what was the sleeping arrangement for four adults and six children? Well, no matter the forecast, the plan was always for good weather, so that tents, and children, could be pitched outside. When that was not possible, Mom and Aunt laid claim to the entire dinette sleeping platform which left eight of us in the back of the camper. We were four girls and two boys. So the girls teamed up, two to a bunk. My brother and my male cousin were stuck bunking with the dads, which always meant the bottom bunk, as the dads were simply not going to scramble up to the top bunks. It also meant that my brother and cousin were trapped in the inside position, virtually pinned to the wall of the bus. With fathers that were heavy sleepers, both boys could be stuck on any given morning for what seemed like an eternity. It was a bit of fun to watch their contortions as they tried to snake out of their bunk prisons around their fathers but without waking them.

As the transition from school bus to motor home progressed, the younger contingent of family and friends lobbied hard for a multi-colored paint job that mimicked the bus on The Partridge Family. A popular TV show at the time, about a family that toured the country as a pop band. But our family was not a pop band. No one sang well and no one played an instrument well. Alas, that paint job was not to be. Ever the minimalist, Pops decided on a simple background of white with the raised panels running horizontally along the side painted a decidedly un-psychedelic dark green. But still, it was one sweet ride. Pedestrians did not seem to know what to make of this striped monster as we floated by, with two or three bikes strapped to the back. After a few outings, it became clear that, once that baby was positioned and parked, it was a massive pain to 'run out to the store' for any incidentals that may have been forgotten. So Pops added a tow hitch and a 1960s Volkswagen Bug to the party. A very boringly beige colored bug. I mean, we didn't need the bug to get attention, but it didn't hurt either.

Now any motor home that is going to allow an urban family or two to pretend to be camping really needed to have a full range of modern conveniences, like a stove, fridge, shower, and toilet. Alas, these were fraught with their own quirks and difficulties, particularly when expected to service ten people.

Somewhere in the undercarriage of the behemoth was a tank for clean water and a tank for grey to black water. And those tanks were finite in size. Consequently, while cleanliness was always stressed for the children, running the water was very much discouraged. Showers were absolutely out of the question.

The toilet was a source of wonder (for the kids) and constant aggravation (for the dads). It was a device that used chemicals to break down the toilet paper and other items that are typically flushed. It was like an airplane toilet, but with a receptacle tank that was smaller than one on an airplane. It didn't 'flush' in the traditional sense, where one pulls the handle, releases it and the toilet knows how to finish the job. With this toilet, you could keep the disposal mechanism working until you let go of the handle, causing an unnecessarily large amount of clean water to be used and unclean water to be pumped into the grey water tank, which was laughably undersized for ten people. Using the facilities while we were in motion was an adventure, although the sheer tininess of the room left very little space around which to be batted. Think 'water closet' with an emphasis on 'closet.' As far as our parents were concerned, though, THEY would take OUR chances with the onboard facilities rather than risk a road stop that could waste thirty minutes or more corralling six children back onto the bus.

Although this was our conveyance to a world of camping and the great outdoors, my parents weren't exactly the type to head out onto the open road with no plans, no directions, and no reservations. No, we stayed at campsites that had words like 'river,' 'brook,' and 'Yogi Bear's Jellystone Park' in their names. To the extent that we children could demand anything, we always lobbied hard for a pool and a rec room with pinball machines (okay, it was the early '70s). And there were always shower facilities to relieve the burden on our practically useless motor home shower, even if the inevitably wooden stall showers rarely dispensed hot water.

When we pulled into a campsite in our giant 'hippie' bus, with a decidedly un-hippie adult at the wheel, we always got more than a few stares. Then the maneuvering started, as we pulled into our assigned spot and attempted the monumental task of parking the thing so that it was more-or-less level. After the VW Bug was unhitched, my father and uncle would begin a delicate dance between man and machine, because each site had its own unique layout and collection of trees, rocks, and other objects that had to be avoided. And why was being level so all-important? Because several of our essential systems and appliances would not function properly if they were not level. The refrigerator, for one, was extremely adamant about this point. The aforementioned water tanks were partial to horizontal as well.

Once we were settled in, it was time to connect to the campsite's sweet electricity supply. Of course, we had very few electronic devices. A television would have been absurd, as reception would have been non-existent. But being hooked into the grid obviated the need for the ridiculously noisy generator and that was nice for all concerned, both humans and forest creatures.

The bus also tapped into the campsite's water and sewer systems. That allowed us to brush teeth and wash hands with abandon. But to this day, I still don't know if this alleviated the complexity of the chemical toilet. That toilet seemed to be a constant source of consternation for the dads.

At the end of every vacation, on every trip home, we children were always a little melancholy. The pothole-induced bumps were a little less amusing. Being pummeled in the bathroom by the motion of the bus became tiresome. The panting and quaking of the dog remained annoying.

But there was still one bit of excitement waiting for us when we pulled onto our street. We lived on a narrow block on the southwest edge of Queens and Pops always backed the bus into our equally narrow driveway. The choreography was delicate and the stage needed to be set in a very certain way. Depending on the configuration of cars parked on the street at the time, one or two of us could be dispatched to ring doorbells and politely ask a neighbor to move their car because the absence of power steering simply did not allow for delicate maneuvering. The telephone pole was a potent obstacle, but we could do nothing about it. And one summer evening, as the wheels on the bus went round and round in reverse and my brother's hand absentmindedly motioned our father to keep backing into the driveway, the wheels on the bicycles strapped to the bus also went round and round, as the handlebars rammed straight through the garage door, signaling to Pops that the parking dance was finished.

ALL THE WAY HOME
NONFICTION
Patty Somlo

THE BED and breakfast where we'd spent the night sat above the shore of the Columbia River. After enjoying a breakfast of quiche, fruit, muffins, fresh-squeezed orange juice and coffee, my husband, Richard, and I walked across the gravel lane to look at the water. Most of the year, Astoria, Oregon was a wet, dreary town. But on this July morning, sunlight sparkled across the mostly calm water.

I was wearing backless sandals, so had to step carefully down rocks that led to the river. The thought of losing my footing made me nervous. But something else was tying my stomach in knots. Since we were out of the city where traffic was light, I needed to take the opportunity to drive.

I was gnawing on my old driving fear, even as I took in the soothing river scene. On the opposite bank of the flowing emerald river were dark green pine and fir trees. I couldn't help but glance to my left, at the Astoria-Megler Bridge that spanned the river, thinking how high it was and long. I was about to drive over that bridge for the first time. As I looked at the bridge, the fear of heights that still plagued me brought on a momentary lightheadedness. What if I got scared halfway across and couldn't go on? I'd been on the bridge multiple times as a passenger and knew there was no place to pull over and stop.

For over a year now, in my mid-fifties, I had been learning to drive. Richard was determined that I should master the necessary skills and gain enough confidence to take the car and drive wherever I wanted. As much as I hoped to rid myself of the phobia that had gripped me for decades, having the freedom to drive anywhere still seemed like a dream. When Richard and I made plans for a practice session, I felt hopeful. Yet when the time drew near, the fear reemerged.

I lingered by the river, willing the serenity of the scene to seep inside my brain and wash away the anxiety. It worked for a time but then the gnawing worry barged back in and sent my mind flying up to the bridge.

"Why don't we get going?" Richard asked.

I reeled my mind back to where we stood on the Columbia's southern bank and reluctantly nodded.

We crept around and up the circular ramp, then I began to make my way across the span. I reminded myself to blink and breathe, while aiming my attention straight ahead. We passed the *Welcome to Washington* sign, and before I knew it, we had come to the bridge's end. The traffic light was red, so I slowed down and stopped.

"You did it," Richard said, and we high-fived.

I took my right hand off the steering wheel and wiped a sweaty palm on my shorts. Before the light turned green, I rushed to do the same with the left one.

For months before and after that day, I practiced. The lessons always took place on back roads. The first occurred east of Portland, on the Historic Columbia River Highway, a two-lane road that ran parallel to Interstate 84. The first time, I wanted to do anything but drive.

A frequently absent military dad and a depressed, anxious mom were two of the factors that contributed to my not having learned to drive when I was young. A phobia set in, which except for one short series of lessons in my twenties, served as a barrier, keeping me from trying.

Several aspects of driving terrified me. Every time a car came toward me on the other side of the yellow line, I feared turning the wheel too hard and plowing into it. This never happened, of course.

The second, more towering fear was that I didn't feel the slightest bit in control of the car. Instead of me driving, the little Corolla seemed to be powering itself. This odd and scary sensation lasted through numerous practice sessions. Luckily, this out-of-control car never got into an accident. Even though I didn't think I was in control, it appeared I was.

My favorite back roads driving occurred in Montana. In those wide-open spaces, the speed limit, even on two-lane highways, was eighty-five.

At first, I was wary of edging close to the speed limit. I had never driven above fifty or fifty-five. But soon I was flying, at sixty and sixty-five, then seventy, and finally up to eighty.

The following day, I found myself driving the winding, climbing, narrow road through Glacier National Park, appropriately named the Going-to-the-Sun Road. I felt as if I were driving to Mt. Everest.

There was just one problem. We wanted to stop and see the sights. Up to this point, my lessons had consisted of straight-away driving on rural roads. I hadn't moved on to parking and backing up.

So, Richard had to take over. He vowed that when we got back to Portland, my lessons would move onto the city streets. Parking and backing up were at the top of the agenda.

Close to a year into my lessons, Richard announced, "We need to buy you a car."

I had never driven alone. Even with Richard next to me in the passenger seat, I still frequently wiped the sweat off my palms, so this seemed to be jumping the gun.

"Why?" I asked. "The car would just sit in front of the house. I can't drive by myself. I've hardly even driven here in Portland."

"But you won't drive if you don't have a car," he argued.

After those initial objections, the idea of buying, owning, and driving my own car suddenly appealed to me. I began to peruse car ads online. And for the first time, I began to visualize myself driving. I also started to fantasize about *my* car. Before we bought the Corolla, Richard and I had considered a pudgy little Toyota Echo, which I loved. But we ended up finding a pre-owned Corolla with low miles, so bought that instead.

Once in a while, I perused the cars being sold by dealers. They were all priced above what I wanted to spend. Plus, I was still afraid to drive on the freeway. So, that forced me to eliminate the dealers only reachable on busy, multi-lane highways.

On a warm, sunny April afternoon, Richard called and made arrangements for us to see a Corolla for sale. From the outside, the white Corolla looked fine. Richard asked the owner, James, to open the trunk. At that moment, James mentioned that he didn't have a spare tire for the car. After James closed the trunk, Richard walked around checking the tires. Even I could see they were smooth, more like the inner tubes we used for swimming when I was young than what ought to be on a car.

"Can I take it for a drive?" Richard asked, and James said, "Sure."

As we were about to get in, James decided to mention something else.

"By the way, the engine light keeps coming on. I don't think it's anything to worry about."

After a short spin around the block, in which the engine light never shut off, Richard said, "I think we'll pass."

In our perusing of *The Oregonian,* I had seen an ad for a Toyota Echo being sold by a suburban dealer.

"Let's go look at that Echo," Richard suggested.

A block before we reached the dealership, I spotted the car. Perched atop a slanted ramp high above the lot, the pudgy little vehicle looked about to take off, headed for the sky.

"There it is," I said to Richard, as he searched for a place to park.

I didn't add what had popped into my mind. *It's exactly what I want.*

Richard got out of the car and walked over to the ramp. I followed. Sunlight winking off the shiny blue metal surface, practically blinded me. From where I stood, the car looked brand new. As much as I judged the car to be absolutely perfect, the price wasn't.

"Do you like it?" Richard asked.

"Yes," I said, almost in a whisper. "But it's too much."

"Don't worry. We can negotiate the price."

We had already spent at least forty-five minutes at the dealership, talking about the car. When it came time for a test drive, I demurred, saying that Richard should drive. Bud, the salesman sitting in the passenger seat, turned around and asked, "Don't you want to drive?" I said no. When we got back to the dealership, Richard leaned over and whispered, "I think we should take it."

Richard leaned into the desk and asked Bud, "What can you do for me on it?"

I swallowed hard. This was really going to happen. We were buying a car. I would have to drive it home.

Bud got up to consult with his manager about Richard's offer.

"I'm scared," I whispered to Richard.

"About what?"

"I'm afraid to drive it home."

"Don't worry. You can do it. I'll be right behind you."

It did feel better to voice my concern. Richard's reassurance, though, didn't change my anxiety. The fact was I had never driven alone. Now, I would have to venture out solo on a busy highway in the middle of rush hour on a road far more congested than any I had driven before.

Bud got up from his desk several more times. I felt as if Richard and I had been sitting across from Bud for months. Part of me wanted the time to drag on, pushing that terrifying drive further into the future.

Late in the afternoon, Bud eased himself down into his chair, looked at Richard, and said, "This is the best I can do."

Richard reached his hand out and said, "You've got a deal."

Bud mimicked Richard, and the two men shook hands and smiled.

As if I weren't terrified enough, before we stepped out the door, Bud warned, "Traffic's too heavy this time of day for you to make a left turn coming out of the lot. You should turn right and go around the block."

The words, *traffic's too heavy,* reverberated in my mind.

Instead of walking toward my car, I felt as I were heading for the guillotine.

I took my time adjusting the seat, testing and retesting that I could reach the pedals for the gas and brake. I spent several minutes fiddling with the mirrors. Richard waited outside, as I lifted my foot to press down on the pedals another time and looked up at the rearview mirror to be sure I would be able to see him in the Corolla behind me.

"Are you ready?" he asked.

"I guess so," I said and swallowed.

"You'll do fine." He leaned in the open window and kissed me. "Remember, I'll be right behind you the whole time."

I pulled out of the lot and made a right turn, checking in the mirror that Richard was behind me. I strangled the steering wheel with my hands as if holding on tightly might save me. Every few minutes, I took the risk and lifted one hand off the wheel to wipe it on my jeans, and then repeated the move with my other hand.

There wasn't much gas in the car, so the first thing I needed to do was find a gas station. A few minutes after leaving the dealership when I was just beginning to settle down into the drive, I spotted a Chevron sign ahead on the right. I put on my turn signal and moved over to the right lane, which I'd been avoiding up that point, because I quickly saw that it became an exit-only lane over and over again.

I eased the car up next to the gas tanks to a location I thought would be right, then stopped and shut off the engine. Richard pulled up behind me.

"You're doing great," he said, his arms around me, pulling me close. "You okay?"

My legs were shaking the way they did after a long bike ride. *Spaghetti legs,* I called this. I was still scared, my throat dry, palms sweaty. But I also felt happy, even exhilarated. I had made it this far. Not only that. I had managed to look ahead on the road and see that I needed to avoid the exit-only lane in time. And I'd found the gas station. All of this boded well for the rest of the drive.

I was relieved that I didn't have to learn how to pump gas at that moment. State law in Oregon prohibits drivers from touching the pumps. I told the young attendant to fill it up with regular as if I'd been doing this for decades. When he finished, Richard paid.

The four-lane highway passed through several small, worn-down Oregon towns, where the speed limit dropped to thirty. We could have taken the much faster freeway but I wasn't prepared for that. This highway was enough.

The road left another small town with a lovely park, a smooth stretch of green lawn that ran alongside the Clackamas River. I snuck several quick glances, gulping up the golden light on the river, then just as quickly steered my attention back to the road. The road had now become lined on both sides by tall trees. It looked like a highway and the speed limit went up to fifty-five.

I was still gripping the steering wheel, sitting stiffly forward. Even though I was going faster here, I began to settle down. I had worried that cars would be zipping in and out of my lane and I would need to watch out for them, but this wasn't the case. Everyone kept obediently moving forward, as if we were all on a conveyor belt.

Before long, the trees disappeared, and we were back in an urban area. Traffic slowed for a stoplight and I did the same. After stopping, I checked the rearview mirror. Richard was there right behind me.

It wasn't long before I finally got my bearings. I was in the city of Portland and didn't have far to go. Cars were zipping from lane to lane, and I paid close attention to the road.

Then I passed Rejuvenation on the right. Richard and I went there all the time, when we were renovating our Victorian house, to buy light fixtures and doorknobs, and gaze longingly at the antique lights we couldn't afford. I was almost home.

Minutes later, Belmont Street came up. I made the right turn and let out a sigh. Here, all three lanes were heading in the same direction – toward my house. This was the street I traveled by bus from my job. Since I wouldn't be pulling over at every other corner like the 15 Belmont bus did to let passengers off, I knew the drive was almost done.

The light was lovely and the evening warm, something Portlanders celebrated this time of year. The traffic light was red at Twentieth and Belmont. After I stopped, I turned to my right and gazed at Colonel Summers Park. People were chasing Frisbees and throwing colored balls to dogs. It was spring and I'd driven my very own car almost all the way home.

I turned right at Thirty-Second Avenue. The street, like so many in our neighborhood, was narrow, with cars parked on both sides. A blue truck was heading my way but the lane wasn't wide enough for both of us. I pulled over to the curb, letting the truck go by, thinking, *I have all the time in the world. I'm almost home.*

I moved back into the lane after the truck went by, drove the half-block to the corner, and made a left turn on Yamhill. My street. Like many of the vintage houses in the area, our Victorian cottage had neither a garage nor a driveway. But I was in luck. A huge empty space loomed in front of our house, big enough for two cars. I pulled in, put the Echo in park, and shut off the car. My palms were damp and my mouth dry. But I had done it. I had driven my cute metallic blue Echo all the way home.

Even though I accomplished this feat, every time I took my car out after that was a trial. If I needed to drive someplace I'd never driven before, I took Richard with me on one or sometimes more test runs. I was terrified of not knowing the exact way to get to my destination, so I needed to make sure I had embedded every turn in my mind.

I had spent so much time practicing on less-traveled country roads that were straight shots from beginning to end that anything that deviated from this pattern intimidated me. Making left turns was high on the list of maneuvers I dreaded, along with changing lanes.

Since I had a dentist appointment coming up, I wanted to be ready. On several Sundays prior to the appointment, I practiced driving over to the dentist's office with Richard in the passenger seat. Like the drive back from the dealership, the route to the dentist's office consisted of busy, multi-lane roads.

Even though I had the route down, I was still worried the morning of the appointment. But everything went well and I pulled into the parking lot and found a space fifteen minutes early. Then I called Richard at his job.

"I made it," I announced.

When I hung up, I realized that I hadn't even thought about the upcoming appointment. I'd had a phobia about the dentist since childhood and normally would have been practically trembling with anxiety over it.

19

RENTING
POEM

Marjorie Maddox

WHO WOULDN'T CHOOSE
    the just-washed white of this Aspire
    scripted with eighteen small
    miles on a speedometer
    that flips its lottery digits
    beside the accordion-stretched map
    we play into each added-bonus
    state of our prize-winning
    itinerary?

All hail Economy
    and her deceptively large
    leg room, her exceptionally parked
    body, her 35-miles-per-gallon city-sipping
    Vroom-Vroom-Vroom!

. . .

Bless her undented fenders,
    her souvenir-proportioned trunk.
    We are old and in love
    with the non-leather seats,
    windshield wipers that work
    up a beat, doors that open each time
    to AAA approval.

If we drive long enough
    across this uncalculated country,
    how can she not follow us home?
    How can she not, remembering
    the miles of our affection,
    forget how little we paid?

20

WHEELS OF LIFE
NONFICTION
Stanley L. Klemetson

MANKIND HAS USED a variety of methods for measuring the passing time—calendars, birthdays, full moons—but my time has been marked by the wheels in my life. It is not a uniform measure of time, but it does represent periods that are significant to me.

I was my parents' first child, and my 19-year-old mother pushed my stroller on the rough gravel streets of southern California while I giggled and cooed to my admirers. A few years later, I was the one pushing my younger sister in that same stroller. Later, it would be a "Radio Flyer" little red wagon.

The red wagon brought independence that allowed me to collect soda pop bottles to redeem at two cents each or walk the neighborhood selling my mother's paperback novels that I assumed she no longer needed. I roamed the neighbors' barns and sheds to bring home "treasures," including a bird nest and a headlight from a Model T.

When I moved up to a "big-boy" bike, I roamed the streets and alleys of our small town with my groups of friends, sometimes with another person riding on the handlebars. Our scavenging activities took us to the city dump a mile or so outside of town. We brought home new treasures that had been thrown away by others and entertained ourselves by chasing the rats that roamed the dump.

When I turned 16, my father taught me how to drive his 1937 International stick-shift pickup in the hills of Berkeley. It was old, small, and a rusty green, but it was the first of my motorized sets of wheels. The childhood games were starting to pass with the new-found freedoms of a driver's license. We search junk yards for radio equipment to support our growing interest in ham radio. The pickup made swimming, baseball, basketball, and friends possible without a parental escort, but as happens in most young men's lives, our interests moved to girls.

It was almost Valentine's Day, and Frank, my guitar-playing friend, wanted to double date since he did not have access to a set of wheels. Since I had never invited a girl for date, he said he would introduce me to a pretty girl he knew, Peggy. We loaded our guitars in the back of the pickup truck and drove up a remote hilltop in El Sobrante.

The girl that answered the door was beautiful with her soft argyle sweater, long dark hair, and a pretty smile. She didn't know that she was my intended date for the Valentine's dance in a few weeks when she accepted our invitation to go to a guitar jam session in the next town. I lost my nerve to ask her that night. A few days later, our respective high school basketball teams were competing at her high school, and she joined me on my side of the gym. I still didn't ask her to the dance and neglected to offer to drive her home. My mistake, because my interest in fast wheels netted me a ticket for drag racing after the game.

A few days later, I got up the nerve to ask her to the dance, and she accepted. Mission accomplished – a date and a set of wheels. But I had not thought of the practical side of the plan. The 1937 International pickup with its small cab was a challenge for double dating. The gear shift was on the floor in the middle of the cab. Afraid that I would grab her knee rather than the gearshift knob when I tried to drive, I sat next to the gear shift with Peggy between the steering wheel and door. Frank and his date sat on the other side of the gearshift. It was a cozy ride to the dance, but none of us complained. The community center was beautifully decorated for the dance, and my date was even more beautiful. This was the start of our dating with its normal ups and downs.

By the middle of my senior year, Peggy and I had broken up, and I became involved in senior year activities like sports, dinners, dances, and the Senior Ball. It was mid-summer after graduation that I decided to host a beach party on the California coast. I had convinced my father to buy a 1952 Ford sedan for $250 so I would have something nice to drive to the beach party. As luck would have it, my father and I were building a small store on the corner of the street that Peggy had to walk past to get to her home, and she would visit us sometimes.

My father said to me, "Why don't you date a nice girl like Peggy?"

I didn't go so far as to ask her out again, but I did invite her to the beach party.

I led the caravan to the beach, but I had forgotten the name, so after a few wrong stops we finally got to San Gregorio Beach. The parking was on a beach overlook, and we had to carry the food down the steep trail. Being creative young men, we decided tossing the food over the edge to waiting hands would be easier. I threw down a 10-lb box of hotdogs, but it slipped through the hands of my receiver, dropped to the sand, and broke open. We had to eat sandy hotdogs all day, but we did eat them. Peggy had not come with a date, and before the day was over, I had my head in her lap playing my guitar as if we had never been separated. She did ride home with me that day.

I bought my own set of wheels after high school. It was a Hillman convertible that needed to be painted, but I had the title. I pampered it and made great plans to make it beautiful as I drove it in the California sunshine. I selected a metallic blue paint, but I needed to prepare the body. Peggy helped me strip the old paint and sand out the rough spots. When it was ready, I parked it in the driveway and with a borrowed paint sprayer, I applied the beautiful metallic paint. The metallic specks were not uniform, but it was still a pretty car. I didn't learn until later that you must keep the metallic particles mixed while spraying.

I was proud of my car even it had some small problems, including an oil leak.

I was in college and had little money. Peggy and I had been engaged for over a year. One day, I happened to mention to Peggy that if she had a job, we could get married. That day, she used my car and found a job. Unfortunately, I neglected to remind her to check the oil. It ran out when she was driving it, ruining the engine. I lost a car but got a wife. It was a good trade.

21

THE FIRST TIME I SAW HER
NONFICTION
S.L. Clarke

I KNEW it the first time I saw her. I *wanted* her. She had definitely been around the block a few times, but she'd been well taken care of and hardly showed her age. I've always liked the idea of love at first sight, but I never thought it would happen for me. Her curves enticed me, revealing strength yet also softness.

Conformity, but with attitude.

Until that moment, I hadn't noticed any other that was as beautiful. Yet after that first sight, I saw copies all over the place. Like the reflection of her silhouette burned into my retina from staring too long. She was encased in a beautiful coat. It glimmered as I approached her, an astonishing shade of blue.

Electron Blue, I would later discover.

I tuned out the prattling of her current guardian as I circled her. I could not get enough of the radiant blue hugging her curves.

"Wanna take it for a drive?" the seller asked.

It?

"Sure," my husband said, holding out his hand.

Keys jangled and plopped into Justin's palm. I got in the passenger seat. I wanted to drive her first, but I was nervous, as if I would mess something up, say the wrong words.

I didn't want to move the relationship too quickly.

I was so shy and uncertain, whereas she was bold and confident. Rather than a match made in heaven, it seemed more like a disaster waiting to happen.

Justin got behind the wheel and adjusted the seat. While he acquainted himself with the levers, knobs, and buttons, I fidgeted, too, running my hand over the newly cleaned interior and memorizing the position my arm took when rolling down the window or opening the door.

My parent's white Accord sat in the driveway as if abandoned. We had borrowed that after our Civic got totaled in a blizzard. My parents were as conservative as their car choices. Long lasting Hondas, bland colors. Blend in. Don't stand out. Don't make waves. Those were lessons that still haunted me, hiding my hellish childhood.

In the passenger seat, I felt awkward and uncertain; I felt empowered and secure.

She smelled of old cigarettes, and I found an empty pack stashed away. The current owners seemed as religious as my parents and had already commented that it wasn't really their car but their son's. I wondered if they knew he smoked. I decided not to mention it.

Justin put the key in the ignition and the engine came to life. She was finally speaking to me. My heart sang.

"Ready for this?" Justin glanced at me.

I nodded, grinning.

It was a short drive through the neighborhood, and yet it was forever. Forever until Justin pulled over and we switched places. I tested the distance between the pedals and their give before moving her out of park. Her smooth wheel spun under my palms.

"I like that it's got four-wheel drive," Justin commented. "And the anti-lock brakes."

Considering that the lack of them totaled our last car, I was grateful for them as well, but I was hardly listening to his review as he continued talking about the full spare mounted on the back. He liked her because of the functionality. I loved her for her attitude.

She didn't have a loud or powerful engine, but I could tell there was strength to her. A strength that I envied. She seemed to say, "I am daring and different, and I don't care what you think of me," as I drove her past bland colored cars parked in their driveways next to their overly-stylish houses. Prim and perfect. Like my parents wanted me to be. But I wanted to be more like *her*.

By the time we returned to haggle over the price, I knew her name.

Isabelle.

22

FULL FENDERED
POEM

Michael Langtry

SHE'D BEEN LEFT out for years,
    parked where rust and dust
    coated her paint,
    but her full fenders,
    round red tail lights,
    twin bumper guards
    still sparkled, and were smooth,
    deep to the touch.

This beauty was equipped
    with a starter button and battery,
    both dead from neglect.
    Luckily she could be crank started
    In a couple of tries,
    and she came to life with a low moan,
    began to shake so
    that I turned her off

and checked her fluids,
timed the ignition,
filed the points, and after one
crank she hit on all cylinders.

This old gal wanted some open road,
     so I eased her out of the flower bed
     she'd been adorning
     and over the curb onto the street
     to the highway. Her big tires
     held tight, screaming
     as she tightly hugged the curves.
     The wind in her grille made
     little whistling sounds.
     And when we returned,
     heated and dripping oil,
     she was ready for a good polishing
     and a garage of her own.

23

CEMENTED
FICTION
Keri Montgomery

TOM LISTENED to the hum of the car—the only artificial sound in the clear Wyoming night air. The brand new 1968 Dodge Charger announced its presence, popping and purring over the gravel as he scanned for late night witnesses on the backroad.

His hands white-knuckled the steering wheel, each heartbeat racing in sync with the engine's pistons. He wanted to open up the muscle car, let it roar like a lion and live. Instead, in the dark, he crawled along while the 426 Hemi growled in protest. It wasn't fair to hold back such a car from its own nature. By design, the '68 R/T Sports Hardtop was meant to be heard. Admired. Drooled over. The metallic blue paint. The smooth blue leather interior with black-stripped seat creases. The sleek chrome center console and matching finishes. It was all meant to be noticed. But not tonight.

Tonight, it needed to be silent. And forgotten.

And so did he.

Tom drove the full length of the road, past farms fields and thick trees, until he pulled in front of the last building before the town's border—his older brother's house. All the windows were dark. The Ford pickup was gone. James was still on his honeymoon. *Good.* Tom relaxed his shoulders. The less James knew, the better. James had bought the house and surrounding eighty acres about a month ago so he and Sarah could start their life off right. James always did the right thing. Tom, on the other hand, was a seventeen-year-old screw up and he knew it. He stared down at his hands. They were shaking.

He steered the Charger around the front driveway and toward the back shop. Then Tom parked in front of the wide metal doors. He turned the engine off, and the hum instantly died. It was quiet in the dark, but nothing even close to peaceful. The heaviness he'd been carrying in his chest anchored in for good. All he could think about was the last few hours. He was so stupid. So wrong. It was all so screwed up.

Tom's adrenaline forced him out of the car. He slammed the door.

On impulse, he stormed into the shop, flipped on the floor lights, and quickly searched for anything heavy. James' new backhoe and tractor were parked at the far end. Tools littered the nearest workbench. Tom sifted through them until his hands found the long handle of a sledge hammer. He gripped it tight, rage in his heart, and ran for the Charger.

The first swing was wild. He smashed down in the middle of the hood. But the single dent wasn't enough. Tom pounded over and over again, swinging the hammer without aiming or caring about damaging the *perfect*. He swung until his muscles gave out and tears mixed with the sweat dripping from his forehead.

The hammer slipped through his fingers, landing on the ground.

Tom stared at the hood—riddled with dozens of dents. He

tried to catch his breath but couldn't. The Charger's owner would've screamed at seeing the damage. But the man would never even know about it. Tom would be the car's last driver.

———

James allowed the awkward silence to swell and breathe in the real estate office. His chest ached, but nothing like it did the day of his heart attack. This was the third time Miranda had glanced up from her laptop and made direct eye contact with him. She sat in her swivel chair, tapping a pen in her fingers, and waited for a solid answer to her question. And this was the third time he'd looked away to avoid her stare. His mind felt numb, distant even, and he couldn't seem to answer. Plus, the pain pill he'd taken before stopping by her office wasn't helping his clarity.

"James, I need your decision," Miranda said. "Are you going to take the offer or not?"

"I don't know." He looked down at the floor, leaning both elbows on his knees. With each deep breath, he attempted to calm his anxiety before it led to another ER visit. "It's a lot of money, but . . . I just don't know."

She let out a soft sigh, then rested against the desk. "James, listen. We've been friends for a long time. Heaven knows we both should've retired a long time ago, but we're stubborn as hell."

He nodded.

"So," she said, "I'm going to be blunt here. You told me you *wanted* to sell your house and farm. You've lived there for fifty years. Sarah is gone. There's no kids to inherit it. You say that you can't handle the upkeep since your heart attack."

"I know. I can't."

She sighed and leaner closer. "This is the fourth separate offer we've had. The other three buyers weren't what you wanted, no problem, but we're on number four now. It's been months, James. These people are offering full asking price. What's holding you back?"

"Well—" he said, pausing. There was no way to tell her the truth. But James knew exactly what held him hostage—a rusted hunk of metal. And he hated it. "I just need to think a little more, okay? Fifty years gives me that right." He stood. "I'll call you tomorrow with my answer. Those people can wait a damn day."

"James, please—"

"I said I need a day."

He hurried out of the office, not allowing her time to respond. Outside, James climbed inside his truck and drove on autopilot, his emotions roasting over their conversation as it replayed inside his head. By the time he pulled onto his gravel driveway and gazed over his eighty acres, he'd cooled a little. Though not enough.

When he got out, he took a few steps toward the house, but leaned back against the truck and rubbed his forehead. Everything felt weighted—his mind, his chest, the decision in front of him. It shouldn't be this hard. He resented how trapped he felt.

The house itself looked dark inside, as usual. And the bushes were overgrown. Sarah never really liked the place. Even after fifty years of memories, she would've told him to move on. He knew it. She was always the resilient one pushing him to stretch. *Let it go, dear. It's just a house*, she would've said. Her voice was still planted in his head, even after death.

In truth, yes, James could picture himself without the old

house and living inside something new that didn't leak or creak. *Modern and Low Maintenance* they called it. Perfect for the retiree in his seventies who gobbled down heart medication with a daily side order of *too-much-stress*. Yes, he could leave the never-ending field projects and broken pipes, but leaving the earth below, that was more complicated. Plus, there was Tom to deal with.

James pulled out his cell phone and called his younger brother. He listened to the rings, wondering how he was going to phrase—

"Hello," Tom said.

James struggled to swallow. "I, uh, need you to come over. I'm selling the farm. We need to talk."

"You're joking, right? I didn't think you would ever sell for real. James, you know what could happen?"

"Yes. Come here. Tonight." He hung up.

Cut your ties, Sarah would've said. *Let buried memories lie.*

Tom lived thirty minutes away in Everton. There was a wait. So James walked around back to the large shop where he kept his backhoe and equipment—the tools that represented a lifetime of sweat and work. But as much as he didn't want to part with it, the shop wasn't what kept him tied to the place any more than the house. He passed the tractor and headed for the backdoor. When he stepped outside, James stood in the weeds and stared down at the ground. For a long while he just stared, thinking and dwelling, and he allowed more raw emotions to roast inside him.

He kicked a rock with his boot, feeling both love and hate for this piece of earth. The space behind the shop had been left empty. Never plowed or tilled. It spanned roughly twenty feel long by ten feet wide, right between the building and a thicket of trees and brush. The area remained secluded and untouched for about fifty years. And even after all that time, he was amazed at how only sparse weeds had grown. It left the rectangle in perfect form—a constant reminder of the '68 Dodge Charger buried under only six feet of dirt. Like a grave.

He gritted his teeth. A vivid memory surfaced of that car in the newspaper pictures. Stories had run for months. The Charger had been the only one of its kind for hundreds of miles —one of 475 that Dodge made that year of the freshly restyled model. People stopped to marvel that car as it zipped by on the mundane Wyoming streets. The owner bragged about his prize.

And then one day, it was gone.

"Took me a while to find you out in the dark."

James spun around, noticing his brother for the first time.

Tom stood near the shop's back door. He flipped on the outside flood light. "Let's talk in the house."

"But the problem is out here," James said, pointing sharp at the dirt. "Here is where it started ruining my life."

Tom's face stiffened. "Ruining *your* life? Your life has been good. The farm. Sarah. Living in peace."

"Not *peace*. That car must come up."

Tom stepped toward him. "But it will destroy me. Everything I've built will be gone."

"Maybe not."

"Maybe yes!" Tom smacked his chest. "You can't predict what'll happen. You don't even have a plan. What are you going to do, James? Dump it somewhere and hope for the best? Hope no one sees an old man towing a rusted classic muscle car and asks about it? You can't be serious. This whole town knows us! And they all remember the story about that car."

In the flood lights, James noticed how tight Tom's jaw clenched and his neck muscles bulged. A full career in law enforcement showed in Tom's fit body, even in retirement and collecting a police pension. In those muscles, there were decades of adrenaline chases, arrests, protecting citizens, and solving crimes. But James knew his once scrawny little brother never unearthed his own secret for the world to judge. Tom never had a plan for the car either.

A familiar ache stung inside James' chest. "Tom, I can't live here forever," he said. "And when I'm gone, I can't protect the car or you anymore."

Tom shook his head. "But you know I can't take over your farm. I can't move. Maryann will wonder why she's being forced to give up her home in Everton. And even if we dug up that damn thing, where would we put it that no one would ask questions? I've gone over this a thousand times in my head. It just needs to stay buried!"

"I can't control where the new owners dig!" James shouted. "It's only six feet down. Did you think of that in the thousands of times in your head? Well, I have. And I was stressing over it right before my heart gave out. The problem is you don't think enough!"

"What the hell? Don't start this argument again. Once in fifty years was enough already. And the sucker punch was enough too."

"It was involved in a crime!" James squared his body, pointing fast at the house. "You brought that to my home." His heart pounded. "You were reckless!"

"I told you, I only knew my friends stole it!" Tom glanced around quick and lowered his voice. "I didn't know they'd robbed that Everton pawn shop after their stupid joy ride. I didn't know they'd shot anyone. Bobby said to get rid of the car. I was young and I was stupid. He was my best friend!"

James' palms felt clammy, but his forehead steamed red hot. "They left you with it, you idiot. And left town. Yes, you were stupid. You buried that muscle car in *my* ground while I was gone on my honeymoon, Tom. Great wedding gift! You deserved that sucker punch. And I have a right mind to give you another!"

"Go ahead. But it won't change anything."

James squeezed his fists and stepped closer to his brother. "I've held my tongue for a lifetime. I lied to the police long ago. To Sarah. Hell, I lied to myself. And I let us walk around like idiots and not once talk about it. But that damn thing has been in the back of my mind every day."

"What do you expect me to do?" Tom asked. "*You* demanded I get my life together. Well, I did. I was a police chief for years. Served for a lifetime. You want to erase all that for a rusted old car that should stay buried? It was a kid's mistake! But people won't see it that way now."

"That pawn shop clerk nearly died!" James shouted. "Everyone was looking for that Charger. It's now a damn legend in Everton. And it's been on my farm the whole time." He smacked his fist into his hand. "I still wonder if you were with them that day. Hiding under one of those masks."

Tom leaned close, his gaze cold and rigid. "I . . . said . . . I . . . wasn't."

James' whole body tightened.

"Leave that car buried," Tom said.

"Give me one good reason why I should."

"Sarah would've told you to."

James recoiled, rage and impulse radiating from his core. His fist made contact with Tom's jaw—fast, direct, and knuckle-breaking. Pain shot from his fingers up his whole arm.

Tom snapped back. He staggered and steadied. Then he lunged, tackling James to the ground.

Before James could cry out, he tasted dirt in his mouth. His right hand throbbed, and Tom forced him on his stomach in submission.

"What the hell are you doing!" Tom shouted.

James swung wild with his free arm. "Get off of me or I'll hit you again!"

"Stop fighting me."

"Or what! Are you going to cuff me, officer? How about you cuff yourself."

Tom let go. He shifted and sat in the dirt.

For a moment they just stayed there. Silent. Cold. James rested his head on the ground, his heartbeat thrumming in his ear.

"I don't want to fistfight you," Tom said. "You're an old man. I'll hurt you."

"It's too late. You hurt me fifty years ago." James glanced up. His punch had caused Tom's lip to bleed.

"I didn't want to hurt you," Tom said.

"You didn't care."

"I did! But—" Tom wiped the blood from his lip.

James sat up. "Tell me the truth. For once. The exact truth. Were you at the pawn shop?"

Tom looked away.

"Come on. You owe me . . . everything."

"I . . . was there."

The strength drained from James' body, and he felt as though he could sink right into the ground. "And who shot the clerk?"

"It was an accident."

"Whose accident? Whose?"

Tom looked away again, tears beading up in the corners of his eyes.

"Whose accident?" James repeated.

"Mine. Bobby and Frankie just wanted to steal the car for a bit. Just a joy ride is all. Then we got to the pawn shop and . . . things just kinda . . . escalated. Bobby told me the gun wasn't loaded. It was just to scare the clerk. I didn't even realize how tight I was gripping until it went off. I can still hear it all in my head. And see it. Smell it. Feel it. And the panic."

Dread filled James' chest, rooting inside his stomach. He forced himself to blink, to breathe, but he couldn't look at Tom any longer.

So he got up. His right hand was starting to swell.

Tom didn't say anything.

"I want the car gone." James headed for the shop. "I have to give my answer about the offer tomorrow."

"I can't move the car. But . . . I could cement over it or something. I don't know. Give me time to figure it out."

"You've had fifty years!" James yelled, gripping the door-frame. "You're old too. You think a layer of cement is going to fix everything?"

"At this point," Tom said, his body drooping and his words slow, "nothing will. I screwed up. You want me to keep saying it? I will. A thousand times for you. I'm guilty. Of all of it. I've been trying to repent to Everton ever since." He stood and walked past James. "Sell the farm. The car will be found. I will confess. And that will be the end of it."

He left, the shop door swinging in his wake.

James stood in the dark, both hurt and numb at once. He was old and wrinkled, but inside him, standing there, James felt the same as he did years ago—the sting of a bruised hand, a broken brother, and a buried car. The rusted metal ate at him from its grave, like his own tell-tale heart waiting for the day his body would implode under the weight, and force James to be buried right alongside the damn thing.

The hurt was fresh, again. Raw, again. Sarah's voice played inside his head, *let buried memories lie.* But he knew they couldn't. Not now. Not forever. It would come up. And with it, questions would be asked. People loved a mystery. The lies would unravel. Wyoming didn't have a statute of limitations for what his brother did. James thought of Tom's wife, Maryann. She was so innocent and clueless that she'd married the man who shot her cousin all those years ago. How would his kids feel when they found out their dad had lied? And Everton? And the police department? Tom retired with honor. And the clerk? He was still alive and long retired as one of Everton's successful mayors.

Tom would go down.

That scrawny little kid. The one whom James had protected from childhood bullies and tended to after skinned knees and bee stings.

"Just let the Charger come up."

James glanced at the doorway to find Tom had come back.

"I deserve it," he said quietly. "I almost killed someone. I can never change that. Or what's happened since."

"No. You can't change it."

"Let it all come up," Tom said, his expression solemn, and looking more like the cop than the kid. He turned and walked away.

James slumped to his knees.

———

The next morning, James dressed in his work clothes and sat down at the kitchen table, a phone in his left hand. His right knuckles had been iced and bandaged. He planned to take care of his injury the correct way soon, but first he needed to solve a problem. That had always been his job.

"Hello, Miranda. It's James."

"Have you made a decision?" she asked.

"Yes. I'm not selling. In fact, I'm going to stay in this old house until I die. My heart will decide how long that is. I've got too many memories buried in this place. But I need you to do a favor for me because we're old friends."

"Anything," she said.

"I'm sending you a letter in the mail. Don't open it, please. File it. After I'm gone, I want you to read it with Tom. Right after I die, do you hear me? Promise?"

"Of course," she said, "But what's in it?"

"Final instructions."

"Okay."

"And take my farm off the market."

James said goodbye and hung up. He ran his fingertips along the open letter on the table. The words were as clear as his bruised hand could make them—easy to read. They'd need to be.

To whom it may concern,

I stole Ed Fuller's 1968 Dodge Charger and committed the Everton pawn shop robbery. I shot the clerk. All of it. My accomplices are long gone. No one else ever knew it was me.

With his left hand, he drew instructions to the Charger's grave. Then he printed his name, adding his signature, and sealed the paper inside an envelope.

As soon as the letter had a stamp, James headed out the

door to the post office and then intended to buy cement. He planned to work until the ground was coated, and he'd live until his heart gave out. Which felt soon. Heartache was his companion. But Tom would be okay, whether his brother liked it or not. God could judge him. He could judge them both.

INSECT
POEM
Fiona Jones

I AM AN INSECT, carapaced, visor-faced and joyful. Smaller than other travellers, I fight the air's viscosity and feel its every rip and eddy, its waves of coolness under trees and its warmth over sunlit fields and tarmac.

You hear me before you see me, black like a beetle but noisier than a hornet. In crowded, slow-moving traffic, you envy my maneuvers as I slip past you, armoured, masked and anonymous, revelling in my freedom of road.

I am an insect, afraid of rain and cold, vulnerable to my mistakes or others', easy to break or crush. "Give it up and get a car," people tell me...but every day of sunshine tells me otherwise. I am an insect still, faceless and invisible, solitary, content.

ECLIPSE
FICTION
E.B. Wheeler

"That's the third time this trip. Are you ready to admit you need a new car?"

I lifted my forehead from the steering wheel and side-eyed my brother Mark in the passenger seat. He might be right, but I wasn't going to admit it. "The mechanic said it's the distributor."

"Plus, the oil leaks, and the A/C is crap. Face it, sis, this Sebring's a piece of junk. You've got a real job now. You need a real car."

"I only have a real job if we can get to Georgia."

"We passed the state line a few miles back."

I perked up at that. The thick trees crowding the road made every mile look the same to my Midwestern eyes. I thought the green would be a nice change from prairies, but it was dark and smothering like the kudzu twisting around everything, strangling the trees and telephone poles.

I turned the key again, and the car sputtered back to life. "Let's just get to Mason Hill."

Mark smirked at the sound of defeat in my voice. Maybe I

did need a new car. The South was sauna-level hot and sticky, and I didn't want to end up walking to work drenched in sweat thanks to the Sebring.

The next morning, I came out of my bedroom and almost tripped over Mark sitting on the floor with his laptop open.

"We're going to find you a sweet set of wheels," he said.

I rolled my eyes. "I think I need a table and chairs first." Everything I owned from grad school had fit in the back of the Sebring.

"That stuff's boring. I'm car shopping."

"Whatever." I glanced over his shoulder at the classifieds. "Something reliable. A Honda, maybe."

He gasped and showed me the screen. "This one! 1999 Mitsubishi Eclipse GSX." His eyes had the dreamy look normally reserved for hot co-eds.

"That's older than the Sebring!" I glanced at the price. It seemed reasonable. Too reasonable. "Are Mitsubishis even any good?"

"They were in the 90s, and this one has less than 70,000 miles. We at least have to go see it. You drive stick, right?"

"Yeah. But, less than 70,000 miles on a car that's more than 20 years old? Did Grandma only drive it to church on Sundays?"

"If she did, she's the coolest grandma in Georgia."

He showed me a picture of the car, seductive curves with a sassy little spoiler, all in cherry red. "You know I'm here to run the library, right? What kind of librarian drives a car like that?"

"The coolest librarian in Georgia." He grinned.

I laughed. "We can look, but there must be something wrong with it. In the meantime, I'm putting your muscles to work helping me get some furniture in here. That's why you came to help me move, right?"

"As long as I get to test drive the Eclipse."

———

The woman selling the Eclipse definitely wasn't a grandma. Her conservative suit and non-nonsense ponytail put me at ease, though there was a deep sadness in her eyes that made her look worn out.

"You're here about the car?" she asked in a soft drawl.

I nodded. Mr brother bounced on his toes. She led us to the garage and clicked it open. The door slowly rose to reveal the sleek lines of the Eclipse. Its headlights faced us, and I tilted my head to study it. When we were kids, Mark and I tried to decide what "mood" cars were in. The Eclispe looked broody, determined, like a Byronic hero with something serious to say.

Mark was busy inspecting the interior. I ran my fingers over the smooth finish. "It's in beautiful condition."

I had been talking mostly to myself, but the woman replied.

"It was my sister's. She loved it." Her eyes filled with pain, but the corner of her lips curved in a sad smile. "She wouldn't want it to keep sitting here and get dusty, and I don't have the heart to drive it."

"I'm sorry," I said, desperately wanting to ask more, but not willing to intrude.

The woman seemed to shake herself out of the past. "Well, it's been five years. Stacy isn't coming back for it." She cleared her throat. "She was only the second owner. It was her graduation present. She changed the oil every three months, rotated the tires... She always took good care of everything." Her gaze drifted into the past again, and I watched my brother play around in the driver's seat to avoid trespassing on her thoughts. "I've done some routine maintenance on it," the woman added, "but it probably needs a tune up."

"May we take it for a test drive?" I asked.

She nodded and handed me the key. The keychain included a carved wooden fob with a folksy painted chicken.

I shooed my brother out of the way and slid into the driver's seat. The leather was a little worn but didn't have any cracks. The seat was already in the perfect position. I tested the clutch and then eased the Eclipse out of the garage and onto the rural road.

The trees flashed by, and the A/C blasted blessedly cool air through the car. I glanced around for patrol cars then sped up. The car zipped around the turns, hugging the road. I grinned and glanced at Mark, who smiled broadly.

He clicked on the radio and tried the channels. Static. Static. Static. Finally, it locked onto a country station. I cringed a little, but we were out in the boondocks. And a bad radio was a small price to pay for a car that felt so good to drive.

When we pulled back up, I hopped out and found the woman watching us, her arms crossed tightly over her chest and her eyes red-rimmed as though she had been holding back tears.

"I'll take it," I told her.

She smiled sadly again. "You look good behind the wheel. I think Stacy would want you to have it."

———

Mark left—after helping me squeeze a little furniture into my townhouse—and I fell into the daily routine of a librarian. I did not feel like the coolest librarian in Georgia as I reviewed library policy, soothed hurt feelings between my staff, or tried to stretch the budget to expand our collections, but when I settled behind the wheel of the Eclipse and flipped the chicken fob aside to turn the key... oh, yeah, maybe then.

I had to drive through a rural, wooded stretch of Old Highway 100 to get home each night. In the daylight, I found the monotonous deep green gloomy. When I had to stay late at work, the dark road made me jittery, not being able to see what was coming around the bends.

Not that the Eclipse didn't handle it beautifully. The only thing I could fault it on was its radio. It only picked up country stations. At work, I could tune to classic rock, easy listening, even a Christian and a Latino station, but in the car, it was just country. The car seemed to like Zac Brown Band best.

I fiddled with the radio, driving through the rain one night. I glanced down for a minute to check the station.

"Look out!" a woman's voice screamed.

I jerked my attention back to the road, where a white-tailed deer stared me down. I slammed on the breaks. The tires shrieked. I gripped the steering wheel and ground my teeth as the air filled with the smell of hot rubber. The Eclipse slid to a stop just inches from the deer.

My heart pounded, and my fingers shook as I peeled them off the steering wheel. The deer flashed its white tail and bounded into the trees.

I took a shaky breath and looked around. If it hadn't been for that shout, I would have hit the deer for sure. But I was alone. No other cars, no joggers, definitely no passengers. I wasn't sure about guardian angels, but maybe I had one. Either way, I vowed to leave the radio alone and keep my eyes on the road.

As the autumn days grew chillier, the trees turned brilliant shades of yellow and orange, bringing the gloomy woods into brilliant relief. The bright colors and stirring of cool weather woke me up on my morning drive even better than coffee. But as the days became shorter, I found myself driving home in the dark more often. I couldn't help wondering what the trees would look like when the leaves were gone and the naked trees huddled along the road in their browns and greys.

One evening after a late meeting with the library booster club, I found myself driving home under a heavy, moonless sky. When I came to one of the many blind turns in the road, headlights flashed in my eyes.

I gasped and clutched the wheel. The headlights veered into my lane. I swerved to the shoulder and slammed on the brakes. The headlights swung in front of me and disappeared into the trees. The squeal of tires echoed in my ears.

I grabbed my phone and dialed 9-1-1.

"What's your emergency?" drawled a voice on the other end.

"I think I just witnessed an accident. Maybe a drunk driver."

Hands trembling, I scrambled out of the car and stared at the empty road. There was nowhere else for the other car to go, but the road was silent. Still. Nothing moved in the woods. The only skid marks on the asphalt were mine. What the hell?

"What's your location?"

I stared down at my phone.

"Ma'am?" the voice drawled.

"I... I'm sorry. I guess he spun around and drove off. I didn't get a lisence plate or anything."

"We'd still like to send someone out to check on things."

"Okay." I gave her my rough location and hung up. The trees crowded along the road, mocking me.

I glanced back at the car. For a moment, I thought I saw someone staring back at me from the passenger seat. Wide, dark eyes watched me from a too-pale face framed by long, brunette hair. I dropped my phone, wincing at the sound of the case hitting the pavement. My mouth was too dry to swallow. I scrambled for my phone and used the flashlight to peer into the car.

Nothing.

Headlights flashed over me, and I jumped. It was the officer. He got out of his car and—for just a heartbeat or two—stared at the Eclipse. His expression was hard to read, but I didn't think he was happy to see the car. It was probably a ticket magnet, all that cherry red. Finally, his attention rested on me.

I described what I'd seen. He took notes, but I could tell by the way he kept glancing at me that he was checking up on me as much as the vanished car. Luckily, it was dark enough to hide the humiliation burning on my cheeks.

When the interview was over, I eased back into the driver's seat. My hands were clammy on the steering wheel as I pulled back onto the road. Zac Brown Band played on the radio.

————

The next week, I had to stay late again. I didn't think much of it until I reached that blind bend in the road. I slowed down. Headlights washed over me. The oncoming car veered into my lane. I slammed on my brakes. The other car spun to the side, tires screaming against the asphalt.

Then it vanished.

It was exactly like last time. Like I was watching a movie. Maybe a hologram projection? Some kind of sick joke? Prickling hot with anger, I swung the door open and stepped out, holding my cell phone up for light.

Nothing.

A projector would leave a beam of light coming from somewhere, right? I scanned the trees. No sign of movement. No obvious place for a projector to be hiding.

"You're not funny!" I shouted at the darkness.

I could call the cops again, but I didn't think they would take me seriously. More likely give me a breathalyzer test and put me on some watch list. I turned back to my car and glimpsed a pale face watching me from the passenger seat. Then it, too, disappeared.

I scanned the trees, but there was no sign of the image being broadcast from anywhere.

With unsteady hands, I started the car, but I found it hard to get to sleep that night in my muggy apartment.

Things always looked different by daylight, so in the morning, I slowed down when I reached that curve. This time, I was coming from the direction of the vanishing car. I pulled over on the shoulder of the curve, turned down the country music, and sat, gripping the steering wheel and studying the road. In the morning sunshine, this looked like an even less promising location for some kind of special effects prank. The trees grew thick and hung with kudzu. The woods would not be easy to walk through, much less to maintain equipment hidden in the trees. And for what purpose? If this was a common occurrence, no doubt the police would have heard about it before now. I didn't think the entire town cared enough about a new librarian to put on some kind of elaborate hazing.

So, what had I witnessed?

At the library, when I should have been working, I googled Old Highway 100. If anything strange happened on the road, there would be an article or blog post. But all I pulled up were occasional real estate listings. No mention of accidents or pranks. No hauntings.

I shivered at the thought, and my fingers hovered over the

keyboard. It was a silly idea, but I typed in "Georgia ghost stories." Of course, this pulled up pages and pages of results. How could Georgia not be haunted, with its long, bloody history and creepy old woods? But most of the stories dated back to the plantation days or the Civil War. A few haunted roadside attractions, but no vanishing cars.

The Eclipse's previous owner had died, hadn't she? That was the impression I had from her sister. I didn't even know her last name, but I typed in "Stacy" and "Mason Hill," expecting I wouldn't find anything specific.

I was wrong.

Stacy Rogers, local folk artist, had disappeared without a trace almost five years earlier. A media frenzy, a large reward, several manhunts, and two psychics had not turned up any hints about what happened to Stacy. After four years, the state of Georgia officially presumed her to be dead.

No wonder her sister decided to sell the car. It would be gut-wrenching to not know. Easier to accept that she was dead.

In this case, I had to admit the sister had made the right choice, because I recognized the pictures of Stacy Rogers glowing from the screen. It was the same face I had seen in my passenger seat.

I quickly scanned the missing persons report. Last seen wearing blue Nike sneakers, jeans, and a sweatshirt. She had gone to a local church where she was installing a painting and hadn't been seen since. Her Eclipse had been found by the side of the road, out of gas, but no trace of Stacy ever turned up.

Cold ran down my spine. I was driving a dead woman's car. No wonder it had been cheap. I felt a flash of annoyance at the sister for not telling me— warning me—but it melted away when I glanced back at the screen. The sister—Laura— pleaded with anyone who might have seen anything to come forward. She had put forward her own reward for any information.

"Someone knows where my sister is," an article stated.

That had to be true. Mason Hill wasn't exactly the wilderness. Stacy just had to stay on the road and she would reach a house or a business within a pretty reasonable walk. Drivers should have seen her on the shoulder.

But the police came up empty-handed, and the news articles appeared further apart as time passed.

"No leads on missing woman one year later," a local headline proclaimed.

She got a smaller mention on the second anniversary of her disappearance. Then nothing for years three and four. Just a few months ago, a brief article announced that the state declared her legally dead. Once again, a quote from her sister begged for more information. The state of Georgia was willing to move on, but of course her family wasn't.

After the sensational headlines, I found Stacy's more mundane digital footprints. Mentions of her art showing at an Atlanta gallery. Social media accounts frozen in time with pictures of Stacy on a local hiking trail, smiling. White pages listings of her former address and telephone number.

I was stalking a dead woman. I pushed the keyboard away, feeling like some creepy voyeur. Didn't it just make it worse for the family when people wouldn't let the dead rest? But Laura wanted to know what happened to her sister, and so did I. I stared at the screen, where a picture of Stacy's art beckoned me. I clicked on the link. Her painting was colorful and homey. Plenty of folksy chickens like the one on the keychain, but also colorful images of children playing in the creek and families working in the garden.

I plunged ahead, scrolling through her social media

pictures. The Eclipse featured in several. I stared at it. It was unreal that I was driving that car. A friend tagged Stacy in a photo from a Zac Brown Band concert. Goose bumps prickled over my skin, and I closed the tab. I was a librarian, not a detective. I needed to focus on my job.

At the end of the day, when I walked out to the parking lot, my gaze fell on the Eclipse, its shiny red body a little surreal next to the minivans and trucks. I wished it could tell me what it knew. How far had Stacy made it after she left the car behind? I slipped into the driver's seat and pulled out my phone to look up the church where Stacy was last seen. It wasn't too far out of my way. I turned on the car, and Zac Brown Band's "Tomorrow Never Comes" blasted on the radio. I quickly switched it off.

I turned off Old Highway 100 to reach the church. I don't know what I expected to find that the police hadn't already, but I almost felt like the car was driving me there itself. I was just along for the ride. I scanned the sides of the road. Somewhere along here, Stacy had vanished. How would I feel if it had been Mark? I bet her sister had made this same drive many times, wondering, wondering.

I parked at the church, the only car in the lot. I hopped out and peered in the windows of the silent building. A painting on the dimly lit wall caught my attention. A dark-skinned, white-robed Jesus presided over a mix of black and white fishermen dressed in overalls, the apostles transported to rural Georgia in simple lines and bright colors. Stacy had talent.

"Who's there?" called a male voice crackling with age.

I turned around and held out my empty hands. A black man in an old suit, his short hair faded to white and a cane supporting his uneven gait, hobbled over to me.

"Is that your car?" he demanded, pointing with his cane to the Eclipse.

"Yes. I'm sorry to intrude. I wanted to see..." I glanced back at the painting.

His face softened. "It *is* the same car, then."

"It was Stacy's."

"Laura finally decided to sell it," the man said, his eyes sad. "Poor woman. And you heard the story, I guess. There aren't many cars like that around here. People remember it."

I nodded, feeling sheepish that he caught me snooping, but he seemed to understand.

"I was the last person to see her," he said. "She hung up the picture for us, and then she was gone. A lot of people came to see it in those first few months. But then they forget. Most of them, anyway. Her family and friends never will. She and Laura had an argument about something earlier that morning. I don't think Laura's ever forgiven herself for it."

What a terrible burden to live with. I had the sense that Stacy wouldn't want her sister to keep suffering.

"I suppose you don't have any idea what happened?" I figured it was safe to rule him out as a suspect. He looked like a stiff breeze could knock him over, and his eyes were kind. The pastor of the church, no doubt.

"Everyone asked me that. I wish I had answers. I wish I could go back to that night. Warn her or something. She drove off just as it was getting dark, and no one ever saw her again. I hope her soul is at rest."

"What if it's not?" I blurted out.

He looked up and blinked in surprise. "Well, I leave judgement in God's—"

"No, I mean, what if she can't find peace because of what happened to her. Or the suffering of her sister. Is that possible?"

"I suppose. I'd like to think that once we depart from this

life, the memories of our worldly troubles fade, but God's ways are mysterious."

I nodded. If haunted cars were any indication, His ways were mysterious indeed. My views on God were a little hazy, but Stacy was making a convert of me as far as ghosts were concerned. I thanked the man for his time and drove back to the main road.

"Is that what Stacy needs?" I asked the Eclipse. "Closure? Did she have a message for Laura?"

I felt like the car was listening. Like it missed Stacy and felt guilty for running out of gas on her.

"The articles said her phone wasn't in the car. In here." I corrected myself, glancing around the leather interior and trying to picture the scene as a woman realized she was going to have to walk for help. "She must have taken it, maybe even tried to call for help. But they never found it and couldn't get a ping on it. So, did someone smash it?"

I imagined kidnappers lurking in the trees. I had already learned in my internet browsing that abductions by strangers were extremely rare—how likely was it that some weirdo spent all his time lurking in the woods and waiting for a stranded passenger to walk by?—but I checked to be sure I had locked the car doors anyway. When I got home, I hurried into my townhouse and fastened the deadbolt behind me. Now I wouldn't have any peace either, not until I knew.

Internet research on missing persons is a dark and slippery rabbit hole. I tried to stay focused on work, but I ate my lunch at my desk so I could browse newspaper articles, looking for just one that might have a different angle on Stacy. My mind kept coming back to it between planning new programming for teens and wondering if I should recommend a better security system for the library.

After work, I said goodnight when the girl at the front desk left, and I stayed at the computer, letting myself slide completely into the swamp of missing persons discussion forums and chat rooms. Armchair detectives speculated about drugs, abusive boyfriends, and double lives, but people who knew Stacy from school or work defended her. She was happy and planning a new show—nothing to suggest suicide. She didn't like drugs because she wanted a clear head. She was wary of strangers and wouldn't accept a ride from someone she didn't know.

The heater kicked on with a rumble, and I jumped, glancing at the darkness outside. I had avoided driving home late at night after the incidents with the disappearing car, but there was no helping it now. If I stayed in the library all night, I would be wearing the same clothes when the part time workers showed up in the morning. I clutched my purse and walked quickly to the car, checking the empty parking lot over my shoulder.

I drove through the silent darkness, the trees close on both sides. When I reached the blind curve, the headlights came. I slammed on the brakes and sat there in the middle of the road. Watching. The car came around the curve. Going too fast. It overcorrected into the oncoming lane. My lane. Phantom tires screeched. The ghostly headlights blinked off.

I got out of the car and slammed the door behind me.

"What does it mean?" I asked the Eclipse. "She wasn't in a car." The Eclipse had a clean accident history, and everyone knew she'd left it behind. Besides, the headlights didn't look like an Eclipse. More like a truck. What was I supposed to see?

I turned in a circle, challenging the darkness. Was it a coincidence? Were haunted cars drawn to me? What a lame superpower.

No. When I glanced at the car, I saw Stacy's face again. Gone when I blinked. But I had only seen her in this spot.

I turned again, slowly, and stared at the place where the headlights had vanished. Something was special about this place. It wasn't all that far from where Stacy had run out of gas. She could have walked this way. It was night. She would have been hard to see. A driver could have hit her.

Surely, they would have looked all along here for the body. The darkness stared back at me, stifling and solid. Kudzu covered everything. How fast would it engulf a body? Either way, it would be easy to lose something—or someone—in the trees.

"What am I supposed to do?" I asked the Eclipse. I wasn't a search and rescue person. After almost five years, there wouldn't be much left to find.

I waited for some sign from Stacy or the car. None came.

The next morning, I decided to be late for work. I stopped along the side of the road where the headlights had disappeared and scanned the ground. It was a paved shoulder, and almost five years had gone by. I didn't know what I thought I would find.

I ventured into the trees. I felt like I needed a fedora and a machete. Especially a machete. I tore away some kudzu and broke a few branches trying to wiggle into the dense mess. I was probably going to be covered with ticks. I kept my eyes to the ground. What would happen to someone hit by a car? They might be tossed quite a distance. I knew from the forums I had read that search parties could walk right by a person and not see them, and they would not have known where to concentrate their efforts without help from the ghost headlights.

Green stained my fingers from pulling away what felt like a metric ton of kudzu. I should have worn gloves. My arms and back ached. This was worse than the needle in a haystack search. Then a flash of something black buried under the green caught my eye. I fished it out. A cell phone with a smashed screen. A cold tingle ran down my spine. It could be any cell phone. Tossed out a window by a frustrated motorist or a phone thief. But I knew it wasn't. On the back, faded from the elements, was a vinyl sticker of one of Stacy's chickens.

I traced the edges of the chicken. This was proof, wasn't it? Whatever had happened to Stacy, it had been right here. Holding the phone, it seemed much more real than it could ever be on some internet forum. Not an intriguing mystery to speculate over endless, but a real, tragic finality. A life cut short, a sister left grieving.

My breakfast sat uneasily in my stomach, but I searched the ground for more. I didn't actually want to find any remains, but Stacy needed closure. I stumbled through the tangled green growth, scouring it for some sign of Stacy.

Nothing.

Was the cell phone enough? It didn't really answer any questions, just proved that she had been in the area. I straightened and craned my neck back to stretch. That's when I saw it. A flash of blue in the dark green of the branches and kudzu.

I gingerly pulled away just enough of the vines to confirm what I saw: a badly faded blue Nike shoe in the tree.

———

The newspaper articles didn't mention my name. I wanted it that way. They just said that a motorist with car trouble (a haunted car *is* trouble) had stumbled across the remains of missing woman Stacy Rogers. After determining that a hit-and-run driver had launched her into the trees, they were even able to match up her death with a DUI stop in a nearby town that same night. The police reported that the pickup truck showed damage consistent with an accident, but the driver didn't remember anything, and there had been nothing at the time to link it to Stacy going missing. Her sister Laura was grieving but grateful for the closure.

The article didn't mention what Laura had shared with me: The tech people were able to get some information off the damaged phone. There was a half-finished message to Laura. Stacy apologized for the fight and wanted to come over that night to talk in person. Said she didn't want to go to sleep angry at someone she loved. Also, they found some sketches of Stacy's next project: a work entitled "Sisters" that showed two stylized women supporting each other with an embrace. The weariness left Laura's voice when she talked about having it printed, just for the family.

I stopped by Stacy's grave to leave flowers after the initial interest had faded. Someone else had left a Zac Brown Band CD. I smiled and got back in the Eclipse. It played any music I wanted to hear now, but I often tuned into the country station. When Zac Brown Band came on, I sang along. And when I rolled down the window and sped down the road, the humid wind rushing through my hair, I really did feel like the coolest librarian in Georgia.

Note: This story is loosely based on a ghost story heard by the author.

26

WILDCAT
FICTION
Matthew J. Ence

THE MAN LOOKING BACK at Tom in the mirror had more gray in his hair than he remembered. He supposed that was to be expected. The last year of his life had earned him a few more.

Tom buttoned his shirt, tucked it into his slacks, and turned to leave the bathroom. A tortoiseshell hairbrush sat next to the sink, Denise's curly brown hair still tangled in its teeth. Tom looked at it, then sighed and walked out.

The bathroom gave way to the master bedroom, the king-size bed unmade, but only on one side. The bedroom gave way to a hallway, which led Tom past another bedroom. He paused, looking through the doorway. It had been Brian's room.

The window blinds were drawn. Thin slashes of morning light illuminated the posters hung haphazardly on the walls. On the ceiling above the bed, tacked flat for perfect viewing while laying down, hung a forest-colored Mustang fastback. It reminded Tom of the one that Steve McQueen drove in Bullitt.

Tom and Denise had drawn the line when lingerie-clad women started joining the cars on the posters. Brian had pushed back, but not hard. He was more interested in the models with wheels.

Tom started to smile, but it felt false on his face and he sobered. He reached down and closed the door.

———

Tom backed his Nissan sedan down the driveway, past the long shape of Brian's car, enshrouded in a form-fitting car cover.

It was a 1968 Buick Wildcat coupe, cream-colored and chromed. The day they had picked it up from the little used car lot in Salt Lake City, it gleamed like an enameled carapace in the cold winter sunlight.

They had loaded it on a borrowed flatbed trailer. He and Brian had both cursed as they fiddled with the nylon tie-down straps. On the way home, Brian insisted on stopping in every little town to check the straps and admire the car. He ran his fingers over the chrome nameplates on its sides. He examined the snarling cat's-head logo in the center of each hubcap as if memorizing its lines. When they reached home, Brian proudly showed the car off to his mother. He started it, and grinned as the muffler-free exhaust rumbled. Denise shook her head and congratulated him, smiling, and stealing from him a rare teenage hug.

Tom forced the memory from his mind, turning his thoughts to the coming workday, its commercial demands straightforward and unemotional. The Wildcat and the burdens of memory sat covered in the driveway, broad and sturdy, and would still be there when Tom returned home.

———

Tom sat in his office chair, the web browser open on his computer. He stared past the double monitors, one displaying a car valuation tool, the other a local classifieds site.

He started at a knock on the doorframe. Eric stood in the doorway, tie askance as usual.

"Hey man, how was the weekend?" Eric said, dropping into a chair.

"Fine," Tom said.

"Did you end up checking out that new Thai place?"

"No," Tom said, "I didn't get a chance."

"That's too bad, man. I'm telling you, best curry in town."

Tom just nodded.

"Hey, you know, the car club is starting up its meet-and-greets again."

"Oh yeah?"

"Yeah, they're doing the next one this Friday over at Worthen Park, like they used to. I heard Stevens finally finished his Bel Air and has been showing it around. Want to come with me? We'll take the Miata," he said with a wink.

Tom smiled. "You know Brian teased me relentlessly the last time I rode in that thing with you," he said. A pang in his chest accompanied his son's name on his lips.

"Alright, man, we can take the 'Vette instead. I think Brian would approve."

Silence stretched out between them. Tom looked down at his desk. Eric fiddled with his tie, leaving it askew in the opposite direction.

Eric finally stirred and stood. "So, anyway, the car club. Are you game?"

Tom thought for a moment, choosing his words. "I appreciate it. This Friday isn't good for me. Maybe next time."

Eric nodded, regarding his friend. "Hey, no problem. I'll hit you up again." Another pause. "Stay strong, man."

Tom watched as Eric left, then turned back to regard the web pages still open and glowing on his monitors. He sat and looked at them for a long time before closing the browser windows.

———

When Tom arrived home from work, he saw a woman standing on the front doorstep. It was his neighbor Jeri. He parked the Nissan in the garage, and turned off the ignition. He wondered if he should pretend he left something at work so he could leave again. He gave up and walked around to the front of the house.

"Hello, Jeri," he said.

She acted surprised, even though she couldn't have missed him turning into the driveway. "Oh, hello, Tom, I wondered if you were home."

"Just got off work. How are things with you?"

"Oh just wonderful, wonderful. I am glad I caught you. How is Denise doing?" There was a bit of buried mischief in the question.

Tom shrugged. "Fine. She calls to check on me."

"Well, I'm glad to hear it. I always loved her, sweet woman."

Tom looked down at Jeri's hands, and took a chance on moving the conversation along. "What've you got there, Jeri?"

Jeri's gaze followed Tom's, and she started as if she had forgotten the dish in her hands. "Oh! I made a big batch of my famous macaroons today. I remembered Brian always loved them, and I thought you might like some."

"I didn't know that. About Brian," Tom said, accepting the offered dish.

"Oh yes, the first time he tried my macaroons it was after I fell in the yard and he was so kind to take me to the hospital."

Tom was confused, and it must have showed on his face.

"You didn't know that either, did you?"

Tom shook his head.

"Well. You remember, when I came home after hip surgery? I decided I wasn't going to let a bum hip keep me from weeding my flower beds. So I tottered outside, and wouldn't you know I tripped over my own feet and fell in a pile on the front walk."

Tom looked properly concerned.

"I know what you're thinking, yes, it hurt terribly. Thankfully nothing broken, but I had no idea at the time and I couldn't get up. I lay there for some time, wondering if maybe I was just going to die there. Well, I heard that noisy car"—a gesture toward the driveway—"rumble down the street, and it turned off and Brian got out, and I called to him.

"When he saw me he rushed right over. He said he would call an ambulance, but I told him no. So he picked me up and carried me to his car, and drove me to the emergency room."

"That must have been when Denise and I were at the coast," he said. "Brian stayed home to work." It was their final trip as a couple, the last-ditch effort to repair a marriage.

"Maybe so," she said, then paused. "Tom, I wanted you to know that I'm sorry I complained so much about that noisy car."

Tom's eyebrows rose.

"Now that I don't hear that engine roaring past my house every day, I confess—" she looked Tom straight in the eyes—"I miss it." She turned to go.

"Thank you for the macaroons," Tom said quietly.

———

Tom needed the odometer reading from the Wildcat.

He went to the driveway and pulled the canvas cover away. From the front, the car was broad-shouldered, the frank round headlamps peering like doubled eyes from its angled nose. From the side, the body stretched for an age from tip to end, the graceful descending slope of the roofline meeting the hump of the rear fenders in just the right place. Partially hooded rear tires added to the streamlined impression. The long tail looked big enough to fit a baseball team in the trunk. The cream-colored paint looked soft, its imperfections invisible in the evening light. It was a beautiful machine, several tons of American steel, forged and folded and molded as a living testament to a bygone age of industrial might.

Tom grasped the chromed door handle, pressed the release and swung the door wide. He ducked his head and dropped into the driver's seat, leaning forward to read the odometer. He jotted the numbers on his hand with a ball point pen, then sat back and took a deep breath. He looked around.

The dash was brittle and cracked from years in the sun. Several buttons were missing from the dash panel, and Tom knew the air conditioning still didn't work, because Brian had been saving up to replace the compressor. He saw the slender auxiliary audio cord that Brian had hard-wired into the radio so he could play music from his phone. He noticed the sand on the floor from the last time Brian and his friends had visited a local reservoir to swim and cliff-jump.

Not long after they brought the car home, the starter had gone out. Neither he nor Brian was particularly mechanical. But after a couple of how-to videos online and a visit to the parts store, they agreed to try fixing it themselves.

They had puzzled over how to get the old starter out and the new starter in. They had argued about the best way to use the shims to get the teeth to engage the flywheel. And when, late into the night, the car started again, they laughed and raised their hands in the air in triumph. They compared grease stains and bloody knuckles, and knew that they had done a good thing together. They were men and they were father and son.

Tom laid his hand gently on the vinyl seat beside him. His son was a man, and he had done good things. And this was where he had last lived.

Tom put his forehead on the steering wheel and wept.

———

Tom's cell phone rang. He sat on the sofa with his laptop balanced on his knees, the classifieds still open in the browser, the form for creating a new listing still blank. A reality show about surviving alone in the wilderness droned on the TV. His cell phone rang again.

Tom checked the caller ID then answered. "Hi," he said to his recent ex-wife.

"Hi Tom," Denise said. "How are you doing tonight?"

"I'm okay. Jeri brought me macaroons."

"And an earful to go with them, I'm sure," she said wryly.

"Yeah," he agreed.

"I came and picked up some things while you were at work."

"Okay."

"I think that is probably the last of it."

"You forgot your brush."

"What?"

"Your hairbrush. You forgot it. It's on the bathroom counter."

"I'll get another one," she said.

"So do I throw it away, or what?" Tom asked.

"I don't know, Tom. Do what you want with it."

Tom waited for her to say something else. He knew she would.

"So, I just called to tell you that I got everything else out of the house. So I don't need to come back."

"Okay. Is that it?"

"I talked to somebody about the car."

"What about it?"

"Well, my dad has a friend who is into old cars, and we were talking and it came up. And he wants to look at it."

"Like, to buy it?"

"I guess so. He wants to know when he can see it. Should I tell him to come by the house, or..."

"I don't know."

"You don't know? Like you don't know if I should have him come by?"

"I mean, I don't know if it will still be here. I listed it," Tom lied.

"You did?" Denise sounded surprised. "Has anyone called on it?"

"Yes. I mean, yes, I listed it, but no one has called on it yet."

"So should I tell my dad's friend to come see it?"

"No."

"Why not?"

"Because...it's not ready."

"What do you mean, it's not ready? I thought you said..." Denise stopped and Tom heard her sigh into the receiver.

"What's going on, Tom? You know that the car needs to be sold. It's the last unresolved asset in the divorce."

"I'll take care of it," he promised.

"How are you going to take care of it?" she demanded.

"I'm getting another call, I need to go," Tom said, and hung up the phone.

———

The buyer called Tom in response to the classified ad, willing to pay full price if the car was in the condition represented. They made arrangements to meet later that evening.

Tom arrived home from work and peeled the car cover back once more, this time stuffing it in the back seat. Tom might as well throw it in with the car, he wouldn't need it anymore. He walked all the way around the car, looking it over, making sure it was presentable.

Tom climbed in the driver's seat, firm and smooth. He inserted the key in the ignition, pumped the accelerator once to set the choke, and turned the key. All 430 cubic inches of combustion engine roared to life like a tiger awakened from a catnap.

The rumble of the machine beneath him awakened a spark in Tom's soul. He grasped the steering wheel, thrilling in the vibrations transferred to his palms. Tom worked the clutch and slipped the transmission into gear. The Wildcat purred, satisfied and free.

Tom remembered the first time he drove the car. Brian said he was too nervous to test-drive it, because he was just learning how to work a manual transmission. So Tom drove, with Brian on the bench seat to his right, grinning with every rev and roar of the engine.

Tom pulled out of the driveway and accelerated gently down the street. The suspension ate every dip and divot, making the car ride as smooth as a boat in gentle waters. Tom thrilled at the power of the big engine connected to him through his hands and feet. This was freedom. This was memory and life.

He looked at the bench seat to his right. The vinyl there was unstretched, the springs and padding uncompressed. But he knew that he was not alone. Brian was here with him. This was Brian's car, but it was also their car. They had bought it and fixed it and loved it together. And now that Tom was driving it again, Brian was there to share it.

Tom pulled carefully to the side of the road and dialed the buyer to tell him the sale was off. Tom was taking the Wildcat home. He was taking Brian home.

27

ICARUS 1981
POEM

Isaac Timm

Seventeen years
his father's pride.

Oh, God
how the girls

would sigh.
As he moved

driven like
Alexander.

Boy not made
for this dusty

dead end, where
nothing flies

but his black
and gold
Trans-Am.

400 cubic inches,
factory prime.

Divine Firebird
pulls easily,

its chariot
past 85.

Smile on
his face.

Hand on his
thigh.

But the desert
tells the truth

well before
it tells a lie.

One blink
turns gravel
into sky.

Oh, God
The sun is

too high.
They say

it rolled four
times

before it came
to rest

his body
thrown

broken on
the earth.

They push
his car

into a pit
for it

had cost his
life.

As far as
I know

It lies there
still,

body rusting
next to

fire.

28

HIGH-CENTERED
NONFICTION
E.B. Wheeler

JENNY and I sat in her little white Toyota Tercel at the top of the steepest hill in Apple Valley. The road was hardly more than a dirt path with patchy alfalfa fields on either side. The Mojave River wove a ribbon of green across the dull brown of the desert below us. Before we had cars, we explored the riverbed on foot or by bike, but once we could drive, whole new worlds opened to us.

"Ready?" Jenny asked.

"Yep." I checked that my seatbelt was fastened and cracked open the passenger side door. I was skeptical of this idea, but I was willing to try.

Jenny cranked up Soundgarden on the radio and opened her door, too. She shifted the car into neutral, and we were off.

The car drifted to the right, so I opened my door wider. The car veered left. Jenny pushed her door out to correct our course. Alfalfa fields flashed by. On the radio, Chris Cornell screamed about boiling heat and dead skies as if he knew Apple Valley.

I had left my stomach at the top of the hill. The bottom

approached all too quickly. Cars zipped by on the paved road that intersected our steep dirt path.

Jenny waited until the last minute to slam on the brakes. The tires sputtered over the dirt, kicking up a dust cloud that drifted into the open doors. We jolted back against our seats and laughed.

"I knew that would work," Jenny said.

I snapped my door shut, dangling my arm out the open window. "Your car's so light. It would never work in the Ghetto Van."

Chris Cornell sang on. The cool evening breeze sailed through the car. The wind always blew in Apple Valley, but it was most pleasant at that time of day, when sunset seeped the heat from the desert and bathed the horizon in color.

"What now?" Jenny asked.

"I don't know."

We just kept driving.

Apple Valley was too rural to traverse without wheels, so most teens of driving age had some kind of vehicle. Mine was the Ghetto Van. A gold 1984 Toyota minivan, it looked (and drove) like a tipped-over milk carton on wheels, and it bore the scars of a decade of cross-country family road trips complete with spilled apple juice, ground-in Cheerios, and crayons melted into the upholstery—smells which were evident when the scorching desert summers toasted the interior. Those might not have pushed it into the "ghetto" classification, but the long gray dent on the side door—evidence of my poor skills negotiating tight spaces in a large vehicle—and the duct tape that held said door closed for some time certainly earned it its nickname.

When a pair of thieves stole the Ghetto Van to use in a Subway robbery—and then abandoned the vehicle two blocks later to flee on foot (undoubtedly making them faster and more maneuverable)—it launched the Ghetto Van into celebrityhood at my high school. The black fingerprint powder never came out of the faux leather interior. I could startle my passengers by pulling the keys out of the ignition with the engine still running thanks to the damage from the screwdriver the thieves used to start the van.

Driving a van meant that I was usually the designated driver. On occasion, that meant hauling drunk friends home from parties. But we also could cram our friends into the van to ditch school at lunch time, or pack everyone and their instruments in the car to go to band practice. The wisdom of giving a sixteen-year-old a van to drive seems a little flawed, but I wasn't going to complain. In a town as rural as Apple Valley was then, driving was freedom.

On restless summer nights, sometimes we would just drive. There was no place to go—McDonalds, Dennys, and Walmart were the height of Apple Valley nightlife. But the desert was out there, empty, unknown, challenging, beckoning. The Joshua trees whizzed by, their prickly arms reaching up in the moonlight, the white sand dotted with sagebrush. The stars stretched across the dome overhead, seeming to promise endless possibilities just out of reach. In the alien landscape, we explored new roads, moving farther from home, but always circling back eventually.

We had to know how fast we could go, and how far, but we also wanted to keep up with the other teens. Along the riverbed, the marks of trucks and ATVs cut furrows into the sandy hills.

"We should go off-roading," I said to Jenny one dull summer night. "It looks fun."

The guys in their trucks did it, so why couldn't we?

Jenny shrugged. "Okay."

I steered the Ghetto Van into the wild ups and downs of the desert playground. We had the hills to ourselves. The van bounced along, churning up a cloud of dust. It wasn't fun if it wasn't a challenge. I went faster, windows rolled down, Nirvana blasting on the radio. We took sharp turns, crested hills into steep drops, and dodged jackrabbits. We were flying in a beat-up old van. For the moment, we could do anything.

A stretch of dry washboard led to a series of low hills. I sped up over the teeth-rattling open stretch. We hit the first hill dead on and jerked to a stop. I pushed the gas, and the wheels spun.

"Huh," I said. "No traction. I think the sand's too soft here."

"Better back up."

I threw the car into reverse, but still we didn't move. Jenny and I climbed out of the van and took stock of our situation.

The Ghetto Van sat high-centered on a rise. We tried putting it in neutral and pushing forward or back. It might have worked with Jenny's little Tercel, but the behemoth van was lodged as firmly as a beached whale.

As much as we itched for something--anything--to *happen* as we cruised the desert roads, now that it had, freedom and exhilaration evaporated into a deepening sense of disbelief and dread. We couldn't move the van, and we couldn't leave it there.

Going home for help wasn't an option. My parents had never *said* I couldn't take the van off-roading, but something in my teenage brain warned me they wouldn't like this. I couldn't risk losing my driving privileges, being trapped.

"What can we do?" I asked.

It was late at night, and we were far from the nearest houses. Cell phones for teens were still a Hollywood gimmick.

"We'll have to find someone with a truck." Jenny perked up. "We should call Brian."

Brian was Jenny's perennial crush, and he had some cute friends he could recruit for a rescue mission. In a blink, the van lodged on the sandy rise transformed from death sentence to opportunity.

We trekked through the sagebrush- and coyote-infested riverbed toward the house of our nearest acquaintance. The night air carried the river's scent of damp cottonwood, but the hills blocked our view of the sandy bed. Rumor held that devil worshippers lurked out there. Without even a flashlight, we stayed close together and walked quickly, not admitting to any nervousness.

At our friend's house, we explained our situation, and Jenny borrowed the phone to call in reinforcements in the form of hot guys with a truck. Luckily, this was Apple Valley, and they were probably sitting around with nothing to do but rescue stranded girls. We waited on them to drive us back to the site of the incident.

"You really went off-roading in your van?" Brian scoffed as he surveyed the spectacle of the van perched on the rise.

Jenny and I shrugged. Some of the other guys laughed, and I only then began to feel foolish for our attempt. Still, we had made it pretty far, it had been fun, and now we had an excuse to hang out with the guys. This would only add another story to the Ghetto Van's celebrity.

Eventually, we had the van back on stable ground, and our impromptu party broke up. We got in our cars, and we drove, glad to once again be moving, even if we weren't sure where we were going.

ONE-OH-FIVE
FICTION
Chadd Van Zanten

ON OUR FIRST road trip to California, I noticed Dad sat a little taller in the driver's seat and drove with a certain extra swagger. I was only nine years old, but it was clear even to me that he had a point to make.

My older brother Marshall slouched next to me in the back seat, dozing with the car's gentle rocking. The travel compass on the dash spun through all four points as Dad steered into a big new cloverleaf and onto the Interstate just outside Flagstaff.

When we reached highway speed, Dad said, "All right, everyone. Look at this."

Marshall jerked awake and together we leaned forward, hunching on the backrest of the front seat to see out the windshield. Dad made a sweeping gesture at something ahead. Mom looked up from her magazine for a couple seconds, then looked down again.

"Look," breathed Dad.

A sunny expanse of Interstate stretched into the distance before us. Nothing more.

"Oh, great," Marshall sneered. "A road."

Some people say the journey is more important than the destination, and there's some truth in that, but in my family it was just a way to hide what we were all really thinking: "We drove all this way—to see that?"

To my dad the destination really was irrelevant. He worked for the Federal Highway Administration, and he may have married my mom, but his first love was the U.S. Interstate Highway System. In our family vacation photos, Dad can usually be seen fiddling with his road map, dreaming about the next on-ramp.

It would be inaccurate to say that we traveled *to* every state, but it felt like we had at least gone *through* them all. Dad's objective was to travel every mile of U.S. Interstate, so where the highways terminated was immaterial—to him there was no difference between a pricey suite in a Marriot Hotel with a view of Disneyland, and a funny-smelling Motel 8 in Squankum, New Jersey. The road was the vacation; the journey was the destination.

"Marshall, this is not just any road. This is Route 66," announced Dad, a little too loudly. "Just like in the song."

"What song?" said Marshall.

"You know, *Chicago to L.A., get your kicks on Route 66.*"

"Sign says I-40."

"Sure, they call it I-40 now, but originally it was Route 66. Same road. You take away a couple inches of asphalt and maybe some sub-bed—same road. Now. Isn't that something?"

He searched our faces in the rearview mirror.

"Boys, this is it," Dad persisted. "The Will Rogers Highway. This is where it all begins."

I wanted to feel something. I looked out the windows, but the Flagstaff stretch of Route 66 was careful about giving up her secrets that day. Marshall and I slumped into the back seat.

Our light-blue '76 Ford station wagon was nicknamed "the Staish." It was ten years old by then but still very sleek, with lots of chrome inside and out. The rear bumper was a collage of decals from fuel stations and souvenir shops. Calling the Staish "roomy" would be an insult to the Ford Motor Company. The bench seats were wide enough to accommodate a modest religious gathering. Two people could take a nap on the dashboard.

Marshall had once asked, "Why's it called a station wagon? It's not a station, and it's not a wagon."

Dad always had an answer for questions like this. "Station wagons were invented to pick up people from the train station, Marsh," he said. "The people ride up front and the luggage goes in the back."

By the "back" Dad meant the place we called the "back-back," the cargo hold, the area back behind the back seat, but we never kept luggage there. Dad lashed our bags to the roof rack with yards of nylon rope. This left the back-back free for us to roam around. There was even a backwards-facing rumble seat, which we pretended was the tail gun of a B-17. Dad always drove pretty slow, so when cars passed us by, Marshall and I would let them have it like they were enemy Zeros.

When the Staish had rolled on for a few miles, Dad pointed through the windshield again. "Okay, you guys," he said. "Look at this."

Marshall and I pulled ourselves back up, more slowly this time. The same highway stretched into the distance, only now it climbed a hill and bent to the right.

"Curve coming up," said Dad. "See the curve up ahead? But it tilts, too. See the tilt? Just a coupla degrees—like that." He held up his hand at a slight angle. "Ever notice how racetracks are banked on the curves? Same thing. That's why we can do sixty all the way through and not even feel it. If it was flat, like they were years ago, we'd have to slow down to forty or forty-five. Now. Isn't that something?"

Marshall sighed and let his face fall into his hands. I read Dad's expression in the mirror and knew he wasn't done.

"Don'tcha see?" he said. "It's American Ingenuity right in front of you. Without that tilt, we'd go flying off the road. We'd fly right off, like a— like a—"

But he couldn't think of anything, so he trailed off and stared out the windshield, his face coloring.

Marshall, maybe feeling guilty, offered what little help he could. "Like a helicopter?"

"No," said Dad testily, "not like a helicopter."

"Like a jet," I corrected, thinking Dad was looking for something with more power, more velocity.

"No, we wouldn't *take* flight. We'd just fly off the embankment and crash."

"A helicopter could crash," contended Marshall.

Dad clicked his tongue and sighed.

"Like a missile, Howard," Mom suggested, without looking up. "We'd fly off like a missile."

"Well, okay, maybe," said Dad. "Missile's a little better. Better than a helicopter, anyhow."

Marshall was fond of helicopters. He glared. "Why not a helicopter?"

"Marsh, it's not about that. It's about the road design, it's about the tilt. Just look at that tilt. Forget sixty. The design speed is probably ninety—we could do a hundred all the way through."

Marshall and I looked at each other. At last, something to work with. Marshall took the lead.

"Could we?" he asked, but it was no question. It was a challenge.

"No," said Mom, flipping a page.

We did not see Dad's foot press down on the gas, but the long needle of the speedometer stirred, advancing slowly to the right, through the sixties and into the seventies. Mom sensed the acceleration and closed her magazine.

"Howard, no," she said.

"Floor it, Dad," said Marshall.

Dad's eyes narrowed in the mirror as Marshall and I hunched forward until we were nearly in the front seat. The engine revved hoarsely, and there was another sound above us. Dad always covered the luggage in the roof rack with a blue tarp in case of thunderstorms. A flap of it must have worked loose because as we gained speed it made a sharp crackling sound, like machine-gun fire.

Mom clutched at the armrest and dashboard; the magazine spilled from her lap.

"Howard," she warned.

The Staish shot past a gently bouncing U-Haul van, put on steam, and zipped by a red sports car, something that had never happened before.

"That was a 280z!" cried Marshall, turning and pointing as the car fell behind us.

When the speedometer needle pushed up through eighty, the Staish began to shimmy. We overtook a Lincoln Continental, but now we were climbing the hill. The old engine struggled against gravity, and the curve was coming on fast.

"Come on," growled Dad. He looked down at the

speedometer, not to see how fast we were going, but to address the Staish more personally, more directly. "Come on, baby."

As the Staish rocketed into the curve, we were pulled toward the driver's side with surprising force. Dad had started out with only his left hand on the steering wheel, using his other hand to gesture emphatically. Now he perhaps thought it would be a show of weakness to bring his right hand into play, and so the sinews in his skinny forearm stood out as he worked one-handed to stay on the road. The Staish strained to swerve straight, cross oncoming traffic, and plow through the guardrail, and I wondered what it would be like when it did—helicopter, jet, or missile.

"Marshall, Nathan," Dad muttered. "Maybe you boys oughta buckle up."

The Staish was fitted with heavy straps that met the technical definition of seat belts, but automobile crash safety had yet to catch on in those days. Seat belts were for racecar drivers and astronauts. Passenger car designers seemed more concerned with figuring out all the different places where little chrome ashtrays could be installed. Our seat belts were used so infrequently they had worked down into the upholstery and were hard to find, and they were used primarily as restraining devices for when Marshall and I misbehaved.

Mom placed her hand lightly on Dad's arm, not to stop him or even slow him down, but maybe for the same reason someone on a doomed airliner reaches out to a fellow passenger just before impact. Dad took this for a signal that the situation was deteriorating, brushed off Mom's touch, and took the wheel in both hands. The muscles in his jaw pulsed and his eyes gleamed, as though he were contemplating the age of the car's Firestones, or the integrity of the rack and pinion, or the half-dozen other components that might choose that moment to fail.

Centripetal force pulled harder as we accelerated. Mom slid halfway across the bench seat and listed so deeply it looked like she was scrutinizing the dial of the radio. Marshall and I gripped the seatback furiously to avoid slipping down behind the driver's seat, but our eyes darted from the road to the speedometer and back.

Marshall shouted, "Faster, faster, faster," but we could scarcely hear him over the engine sound, howling tires, and the crackle of the tarp overhead.

The Staish bucked and shook like a space capsule re-entering Earth's atmosphere. Dad had abandoned any façade of fatherly composure—the car was now driving him and he knew it. He wore a bare-teeth, test-pilot grimace as he fought the car yard by yard until at last the speedometer needle touched the 100 mile-per-hour hash mark.

I knew cars could go that fast, if only in theory. At the speedway we'd seen dragsters go over 200 miles per hour. Even the speedometer in the Staish went to 120, but no one ever knew Dad to go faster than 70. He had done so only once, to race to the hospital after Grandma Sweet had her stroke. I had always assumed 70 was the Staish's top speed and that the numbers to the right were merely to fill up unused space in the instrument panel. Now the needle trembled over the 100 mark and I thought surely the car would speed forward in time, or at least into another dimension.

Marshall hollered, "One hundred, one hundred, one hundred!"

Mom whimpered, "Howard, enough."

Dad did not slow down.

The hypothesis was that American Ingenuity enabled us to

not only reach 100, but maintain it through the turn. Dad knew the exact point where Route 66 returned to a straightaway, but he dared not cheat American Ingenuity out of one single degree of the curve, so he kept the hammer down for another two hundred yards just to be sure. I could hang on no longer. When I let go of the seatback, I knocked Marshall off, too, and we fell together behind the driver's seat.

In the split second before I tumbled down, I saw the speedometer read one-oh-five.

Only then the engine's blast and the squall of tires receded. The blue tarp on the luggage was reduced to an occasional flapping. The transmission eased out of overdrive and, eventually, so did Dad. He took a few deep breaths, and then grinned.

"Like a meteor," he said. "We'd fly off like a meteor."

I heard my mother retrieve her magazine and scoot back to the passenger side.

"Howard," she said. "Just—drive—the car."

Marshall and I lay in a heap where we had fallen behind Dad's seat. The Staish had not shifted in time or dimension, but I felt a new awareness, not only to the physical world, but to the universe of what is possible. Marshall laughed and cheered as he climbed up to his place on the bench seat. I arose cautiously, as though when I looked through the windshield again, everything would be completely different.

It was.

ABOUT THE AUTHORS

Rachel Evangeline Barham is a classical singer and emerging writer in Washington, D.C. She began writing about the confluence of words, music, and experience by creating program notes and translations for her own recitals. Those skills have been honed during a sixteen-year run as the program notes annotator for Cantate Chamber Singers in Bethesda, Maryland, and a position at the now-defunct Music Library at The Catholic University of America. Rachel only recently started sharing her writing, but her essays and personal musings have been published in *Unearthed: The Literary Journal of the SUNY College of Environmental Science and Forestry* ("Coral Reef 911"), Tall Grass Writers Guild's *Loon Magic and Other Night Sounds* ("Timberdoodle Dusk"), and *Chicken Soup for the Soul*. Rachel also released a solo album of American art songs in 2019 (Up Toward the Sky, Guild Records 7819) highlighting the musical and literary voices of women and LGBT Americans, and she blogs about serendipity and ephemera at UpTowardTheSky.com. An insatiable observer, she escapes into the wild whenever possible.

Lynne Burnett lives on Vancouver Island. Publications include *American Journal of Poetry, Arc Poetry, Blue Heron Review, Calyx Journal, Comstock Review, Crosswinds, CV2, Kissing Dynamite, IthacaLit, Malahat Review, Mockingheart Review, New Millennium*

Writings, Pedestal Magazine, Ristau, River Styx, Tamsen, Taos Journal of Poetry & Art, Recenter Press, Underfoot Poetry, and several anthologies. A Best of the Net and Pushcart nominee, she is the 2016 winner of the Lauren K. Alleyne Difficult Fruit Poetry Prize and joint winner of the 2019 Jack Grapes Poetry Prize. Finishing Line Press published her chapbook, "Irresistible" in 2018.

Visit her at https://lynneburnett.ca/

S. L. Clarke is the award-winning author of multiple short stories featured in various anthologies. She dabbled in numerous creative hobbies before landing on writing, cementing her love of stories with a Creative Writing degree from Utah State University (but only because she couldn't major in knitting or sewing). Her short pieces range from personal memoir to fiction, touching poetry only when the muse demands. Her women's fiction novel *True Strength* is set to publish next year. Amid mothering four boys and writing, she crochets, reads, goes to the dojo, binges on Netflix, plays computer games, and sometimes picks up her trumpet.

Neil Dabb grew up in Smithfield, Utah, and has been a freelance writer since shortly after graduating high school. He has been published in a variety of magazines over the years (most recently on Hubpages.com). He enjoys writing, Frisbee (disc) golf and bonfires. He is the father of five children and lives in Logan Utah. Neil presented at the League of Utah writers fall conference in 2014 and LTUE (Life The Universe and Everything) in 2015. Neil has published several novella length books at Smashwords.com (for ebooks) http://www. smashwords.com/profile/view/neildabb and Createspace.com (print on demand). He is a partner at DragonTech writing, a technical writing firm whose mission is to educate companies about what a technical writer does. And you can follow Neil's writing exploits on facebook: www.facebook.com/TheDrag onwritersDen.

Born in New York state and raised in the borough of Queens, **Patricia DiMaio** earned a bachelor's degree in math from Binghamton University and an MBA from the Stern School of Business, New York University. Although she has worked in the information technology space across a number of industries and sectors, she has always been an avid film buff, cook, and reader, and an amateur writer. Memoir pieces and personal essays allow her to communicate chunks of her past to her two dear children, Galen and Bonnie. If forced to choose, her favorite novel would have to be *The Name of the Rose*, which has everything: a mystery and medieval history, herbal potions and philosophical notions, a library and a labyrinth!

Matthew J. Ence is a lawyer and dad whose roots are firmly planted in the red soil of southern Utah. In the last year he's somehow managed to perfect his smoked pulled pork recipe and lose a third of his body weight. He also won't let you forget that Christopher Reeve is still the best Superman. Between putting miles on his bike and ogling classic cars with his teenage sons, Matt writes a few stories.

J Anthony Gohier has been a storyteller all his life. His own journey has taken him through many different creative pursuits including film production, ballroom dance, baking, and game design, just to name a few. However, he has always been a believer in the power of stories to reveal the magic in our everyday lives, and inevitably he returned to the written word. His writing has won awards in several categories, including genre fiction, children's books and poetry. He has authored short stories and poems which have been published in various anthologies in past years. His most recent writing project was a narrative digital escape room, which previewed with a select audience in October of 2020. Jeremy currently resides in Utah County where his day job as a Computer Scientist keeps him busy writing for a mechanical audience.

Janine Harrison wrote the poetry collection, *Weight of Silence* (Wordpool Press, 2019) and poetry chapbook, *If We Were Birds* (Locofo Chaps, 2017). Her work has appeared in *Veils, Halos, and Shackles: International Poetry on the Oppression and Empowerment of Women, Not Like the Rest of Us: An Anthology of Contemporary Indiana Writers, A&U, Gyroscope Review*, and other publications. Janine teaches creative writing at Calumet College of St. Joseph in Northwest Indiana.

Jef Huntsman is the highly acclaimed and award-winning published author of five fiction and two non-fiction books, numerous short stories, and delightful poetry. He was voted Utah's Writer of the Year in 2017 for his Carson series thriller, *Jamaica Rush*, and his dedicated service to the literary community. He spends most of his time writing from his loft, swimming, hiking, or enjoying the peace of raging flames from his under-the-stars firepit at his cabin in central Utah.

Jefhuntsmanauthor.com

Fiona M Jones is a creative writer living in Scotland. Her published work is visible through @FiiJ20 on Facebook, Twitter and Thinkerbeat.

Tim Keller is an avid reader who also has a weak spot for monster movies. He likes traveling, 80's music, and if the highway patrol is to be believed, driving way too fast. After working as a bouncer, mortgage researcher, computer repair technician, caregiver, and a brief, albeit disastrous, stint as a waiter in anachronistic drag, he decided he wanted to be a writer when he grew up. A keen observer of human nature, Tim enjoys writing stories about all kinds of people from all walks of life. His work can be found in various literary journals and anthologies including *Mirrored Realities, In the Shimmering, Between Places*, and the *Helicon West Anthology*.

Kamal E. Kimball is an Ohio poet. On the editorial team for *The Journal* and *Muzzle Magazine*, her work has been published or is forthcoming in *Phoebe, Hobart, Juked, Tahoma Literary Review, Sundog Lit, Bone Parade, Kaaterskill Basin Literary Journal, Forklift Ohio*, and many others. More at kamalkimball.com

Stanley L. Klemetson, Ph.D., (Retired) Associate Dean of the College of Technology and Computing at Utah Valley University in Orem, Utah and currently a civil engineering consultant. He has published numerous technical articles, and has authored or co-authored several technical books and manuals. His literary works have included chapters in *My Love to you Always* (OakTara Publishers, LLC, 2012); *Writing After Retirement: Tips by Successful Retired Writers* (Scarecrow Press, 2013), and *Library Outreach to Writers and Poets: Interviews and Case Studies of Cooperation*

(*McFarland, 2017*). He has finish a draft of a fantasy book, *Ghosts of Emeryville Mine,* and has started on the second book. Periodically he writes short stories, family histories and poetry. Editing and publishing his manuscripts are also his goals. He is a member of the Just Write Chapter of the League of Utah Writers.

Jessica de Koninck is the author of one full length collection, *Cutting Room* (Terrapin Books) and one chapbook, *Repairs* (Finishing Line Press). Her poems have been featured in *The Writer's* Almanac and *Verse Daily* and appear in journals and anthologies including *Diode, The Paterson Literary Review* and *The Valparaiso Poetry Review. Verse Daily.* Jessica leads poetry workshops and is a long-time resident of Montclair, New Jersey, where she is very active in the community. Her M.F.A. is from Stonecoast, and her B.A. is from Brandeis.

Mike Langtry's long interest in cars and trucks and engines led him to own and restore: 1939 Buick Special, 1954 Austin Healy LeMans, 1966 GMC pickup, two Volkswagen Westphalia campers and a Ford 8N tractor. His poems have appeared in *Windfall Press* and *Desert Ramblings.*

Winner of the 2019 Foley Poetry Prize and Professor of English and Creative Writing at Lock Haven University, **Marjorie Maddox** has published 11 collections of poetry—including Transplant, Transport, Transubstantiation (Yellowglen Prize); True, False, None of the Above (Illumination Book Award Medalist); Local News from Someplace Else; Perpendicular As I (Sandstone Book Award)—the short story collection What She Was Saying (Fomite); four children's and YA books—including Inside Out: Poems on Writing and Readiing Poems with Insider Exercises and A Crossing of Zebras: Animal Packs in Poetry; I'm

Feeling Blue, Too!—Common Wealth: Contemporary Poets on Pennsylvania (co-editor); Presence (assistant editor); and 600+ stories, essays, and poems in journals and anthologies. For more information, please see www.marjoriemaddox.com

Keri Montgomery is an award-winning short story author in adult speculative fiction. She's also a contributing author to *Rise Above Depression*, a #1 Amazon bestseller in self help by main author and inspirational speaker Jodi Orgill Brown. Keri's short fiction can be found in numerous collections, including both the 2018 and 2019 LUW Press anthologies titled *At First Glance* and *Metamorphosis*. In 2019, she was a contributing author and main editor for *Spirals—A Collection of Poetry & Prose from Utah's Northern Edge*. *Spirals* went on to receive a 2020 Recommended Read Award from The League of Utah Writers. Keri is heavily involved in the Northern Utah writing community and is the founding member of Brigham City Writers. When not creating fiction, she enjoys museum trips with her kids and wishing for superhuman skills.

Stephen Page is part Native American and part Scottish. He was born in Detroit. He is the author of four books of poetry - "The Salty River Bleeds," "A Ranch Bordering the Salty River," "The Timbre of Sand," and "Still Dandelions." He holds two AA's from Palomar College, a BA from Columbia University, and an MFA from Bennington College. He also attended Broward College. His literary criticisms have appeared regularly in the Buenos Aires Herald, How Journal, Gently Read Literature, North of Oxford, and the Fox Chase Review. His stories have been published in Amphibi, Birch Book Press, Bold + Italic, October Hill, Quarto, and The Whistling Fire. He is the recipient of a First Place Prize in Poetry from Bravura, the Jess

Cloud Memorial Prize, a Writer-in-Residence from the Montana Artists Refuge, a Full Fellowship from the Vermont Studio Center, an Imagination Grant from Cleveland State University, and an Arvon Foundation Ltd. Grant. He loves his wife, family, friends, nature, long walks through woodlands, solitude, journaling, spontaneous road trips, riding motorcycles, throwing cellphones into lakes, dog-earing pages in books, and making noise on his electric bass.

Jack Remick is a novelist and a poet. His work has appeared around the country. Coffeetown Press published *The California Quartet—The Deification, Valley Boy, The Book of Changes,* and *Trio of Lost Souls. Gabriela and The Widow* was a finalist for the Montaigne Award. *Blood,* a companion novel to *No Century for Apologies* and *Doubles in a Game of Chance,* was published by Camel Press, an imprint of Coffeetown. He is the author of two short-story collections: *Throwback and Other Stories,* and *Terminal Weird.* Remick is co-author, with Robert J. Ray, of *The Weekend Novelist Writes a Mystery.* Remick's poetry includes *Josie Delgado, a poem of the Central Valley, Satori—Poems,* and work in *The Seattle Five Plus One.* He has other work in various anthologies including *Raven Chronicles V/ 26, The Helicon West Anthology,* and *So Much Depends Upon,* (a Red Wheelbarrow Writers Anthology).

Marilyn W. Richardson, Ivins, UT, was a dance educator at South Dakota State University in Brookings, SD, a position she loved. Retiring to St. George in 1994, she now devotes her creative energies to writing, another activity to love. She has served as president of the League of Utah Writers as well as being chapter president of Heritage Writers Guild for three terms. She also belongs to Utah State Poetry Society. An avid believer in learning from workshops, she is certain she has attended over 100 of them since moving to Utah. She posts her books on Kindle, https://www.amazon.com/Marilyn-W-Richardson/e/B00MAONMP4?ref=sr_ntt_srch_lnk_4&sr=1-4 and is currently working on an historical fiction about the ballerina Fanny Elssler who traveled to the United States in 1840 —and made lots and lots of money. "I do love the research. And I admit I had to do some to remember more about Khrushchev for my essay in *Wheels*. But it was great to remember that day."

Felicia Rose has published in *The Westchester Review, The Dandelion Review, Mother Earth News, The Way to My Heart: An Anthology of Food-Related Romance, The Sun, The Change Agent: An Adult Education Magazine for Social Justice, The Lavender Review*, and elsewhere. A New York City native, she is now returning home after eight years in Cache Valley, Utah. Because she has become attached to her Subaru, it is accompanying her on the move. Where she will park it once she arrives is anyone's guess.

Patty Somlo has published four books, three short story collections and a memoir. Her most recent book, *Hairway to Heaven Stories* (Cherry Castle Publishing), was a Finalist in the American Fiction Awards and Best Book Awards. Two of her previous books, *The First to Disappear* (Spuyten Duyvil) and *Even When Trapped Behind Clouds: A Memoir of Quiet Grace* (WiDo Publishing), have been Finalists in the International Book Awards, Best Book Awards, National Indie Excellence Awards, and Reader Views Literary Awards. She has been nominated for the Pushcart Prize four times and for Best of the Net once, as well as receiving Honorable Mention for Fiction in the Women's National Book Association Contest and having an essay selected as Notable for Best American Essays 2014.

Isaac Timm was born and raised in the western desert town of Callao, Utah; a stop on the historic Pony Express trail. His highest aspiration is to be a storyteller like his father. He is a graduate of Utah State University in history and English. His poetry and short stories have won numerous awards.

Chadd VanZanten writes narrative nonfiction essays and literary short stories, no one of which is really much truer than any of the others. His fiction has been published in numerous anthologies, including *Creep Factor: Thirteen Deeply Creepy Horror Stories* (Knowledge Forest Press 2018), and in his short-story collection *The Key To This Whole Entire Thing* (Knowledge Forest Press 2019). He is also the author of works on fly-fishing and backpacking, including *On Fly-Fishing The Wind Rivers* (The History Press 2018).

E.B. Wheeler is the award-winning author of twelve books, including *Wishwood, No Peace with the Dawn,* and *The Haunting of Springett Hall,* as well as several short stories, magazine articles, and scripts for educational software programs. She is currently considering buying a 4WD and trying some real off-roading. You can find more about her books at https://www. amazon.com/E.B.-Wheeler/e/B00VKQG6MO   or ebwheeler.com